MERE CHRISTIANITY
STUDY GUIDE

A Bible Study
on the C.S. Lewis Book *Mere Christianity*

By Steven Urban

A Study Course for a Thinking Faith

God is no fonder of intellectual slackers than of any other slackers...Anyone who is honestly trying to be a Christian will soon find his intelligence being sharpened: one of the reasons why it needs no special education to be a Christian is that Christianity is an education itself.

C.S. Lewis
Mere Christianity

Mere Christianity Study Guide
A Bible Study on the C.S. Lewis Book *Mere Christianity*
A Study Course for a Thinking Faith

ISBN-13: 978-1499568264
ISBN-10: 1499568266

To learn more about this Bible study visit www.MereChristianity.org.
To order additional copies of this resource visit www.CreateSpace.com.

Scripture quotations taken from the New American Standard Bible®, Copyright © 1960, 1962, 1963, 1968, 1971, 1972, 1973, 1975, 1977, 1995 by The Lockman Foundation. Used by permission. (www.Lockman.org)

Cover photo of C.S. Lewis used by permission of The Marion E. Wade Center, Wheaton College, Wheaton, IL.
Back cover artwork: *The Apostle Paul* by Rembrandt, 1657.

Version 2

TABLE OF CONTENTS

THE AUTHOR

Steven Urban graduated from the University of California with a degree in Psychobiology before going on to receive his medical doctorate at New York Medical College. He completed his residency training in Physical Medicine and Rehabilitation at Johns Hopkins and was awarded an NIH Fellowship in Stroke Research at the University of Maryland. Today he is a double-board certified Physiatric Interventional Pain Specialist. He lives with his wife and son near Nashville, Tennessee.

Steve who is a native of Southern California, was not raised in a Christian home. While attending UCLA, his life was "interrupted" by a sensation he had never experienced before or even knew human beings could experience. Had that been the end of it, the sensation may have been dismissed as a mere fluke or some twist of the brain, but the sensation returned again and again. As a Psychobiology undergraduate student, he began to search out what caused these sensations. Along with his scientific inquires he also began to read histories, biographies, and treatises on psychology, world religions and theology. He even traveled overseas and spent time in a Tibetan monastery in Nepal. Eventually Steve read a book written by a man which would forever change his life.

The man was C.S. Lewis and in his *Surprised by Joy*, Steve discovered a person who experienced his same sensations, yet did not forsake the use of reason and rational inquiry. The book was the final instrument that led to Steve's realization that Christ was who He claimed to be.

After the four years leading to his conversion, Steve sought out several people and sources to help him deepen his relationship with Christ. Here again C.S. Lewis proved to be an invaluable guide. In *Mere Christianity*, Steve found a wonderful expression of Romans 1-8 leading the believer from compatibility to intimacy with Christ.

FOREWORD

During World War II, C. S. Lewis delivered a series of radio broadcasts on the BBC in England. At the time of the broadcasts the outcome of the war was still very uncertain. People needed hope. Many tuned in to see what this Oxford scholar might have to say. Later the talks were published as the book *Mere Christianity*. Since its publication thousands of thoughtful people have found their way to a faith in Christ that makes sense. Included among these is Dr. Francis Collins, the scientist who broke the Genome, and also Charles Colson, President Nixon's chief of staff, and later founder of Prison Fellowship. *Mere Christianity* is for the thinking person. But the book appeals to the heart as well. In fact, it appeals to the whole person. It is not a surprise that this should be so. In his literary criticism of his friend and fellow Inkling, Charles Williams' Arthurian Poems, *The Arthurian Torso*, C. S. Lewis said, "The first problem in life is how do you fit the stone [the Reason] and the shell [the Romantic longings of the heart]?" Lewis himself came to believe that Christianity did this best. In fact, after his long spell as an atheist, Lewis's first Christian book was titled, *The Pilgrim's Regress: An Allegorical Apology for Christianity, Reason and Romanticism*. He wrote to show that Christianity was a holistic faith that reconciled head and heart. This is because faith in Christ is a reconciling faith. It reconciles those estranged from God into a robust relationship with God. It gives the resources to make possible reconciliation of broken relationships with others. In fact, it provides the means to repair the ruins within one's own life. It sets the believer on the course of reconciling the soul and body as well as the head and the heart.

Lewis is known for his ability to open wardrobe doors into magical worlds where the themes of reconciliation are made accessible through children's stories like the Narnian Chronicles; written for children but very readable for adults. So too, one is grateful when someone comes along and opens a wardrobe door into an enriched understanding of Lewis's books. This is what one encounters in Dr. Steven Urban's *Mere Christianity Study Guide: A Bible Study on the C. S. Lewis Book Mere Christianity*. With all of the diagnostic skill of a physician, Urban offers fresh insight on this Christian Classic making Lewis's thought all the more accessible for those who long to better understand Lewis and his ideas. Urban makes the book come alive with valuable applications for spiritual growth and maturity. In fact the book could be titled: C. S. Lewis's Spiritual Formation for Mere Christians. Urban is right to suggest that Lewis's book is not merely a work in Christian Apologetics and defense of the faith. Its themes are far richer than that. Lewis is concerned not only that the faith is defensible but it is also transformational. This fact is certainly developed by Dr. Urban.

Urban developed this study of *Mere Christianity* while teaching an adult Sunday school class. Over some time he developed the curriculum. Now, his treatment of *Mere Christianity* provides a valuable resource for the Church at large. All over the world Christians have studied *Mere Christianity* in Sunday schools and small groups around the globe. But never has such an in-depth study of the book been developed and made transferable for others to use while teaching from this classic text. Urban has served well all who want such an aid to enhance their own teaching. I have been studying C. S. Lewis for 44 years. I have taught Lewis courses and lectured about Lewis for 34 years at 58 university campuses in 11 different countries around the world. Urban's study of Mere Christianity is the best I've seen. It pleases me to see he is making his own study of Lewis available to others. You see, I've known Steve for over 35 years. My own grasp of Lewis was deeply influenced by things I learned from Steve while I was still in graduate school. It is high time others can have the privilege of gaining from his many years study of Lewis. I recommend the book for all who take their faith seriously and want to grow to be all they can be in Christ.

Jerry Root, PhD

Editor of *The Quotable C.S. Lewis*

Consulting Editor of *The C.S. Lewis Study Bible*

AUTHOR'S COURSE NOTE AND STUDY FORMATS

C.S. Lewis's *Mere Christianity* is now well over a half century old and has sold millions of copies around the world. Yet despite its recognition as a "classic," there is surprisingly little available today in terms of a serious study course that *delves into the depths* of each chapter and in turn into Lewis's thoughts. I have sought here to remedy that.

To follow Lewis's thinking from what our common human notions of right and wrong imply about the universe to the necessity of becoming something like a "new species" of men and women, I first took the Preface and 33 chapters of *Mere Christianity* and organized them into a variety of different study course options (see **Study Formats** on the following page). Then, for each chapter, I wrote questions and cited the specific paragraph(s) from which those questions were drawn (e.g., para. 2 or para. 4-7, etc.). A few questions are opinion-based but most require reading and thought to grasp Lewis's main points and ideas. The questions are also intended to facilitate small group discussions as the discipline of expressing one's thoughts often helps to sharpen and solidify one's understanding. Finally, **Appendices for 'Further Up and Further In'** were added at the end to supplement and further clarify certain topics. The course can be completed singly by an individual, but I strongly recommend that he or she periodically discuss what is learned with another person.

I would also encourage you to visit **www.MereChristianity.org**. This website has been created to offer you an opportunity to participate in open discussion on the book and study. In addition, you will also find an **Answer Guide** to the questions found in this study.

While broaching topics like other religions, morality, evolution and sex, it is unlikely that everyone will persistently see eye to eye. This can potentially cause the question-generated discussions to become rather lively. It is advisable, therefore, that the discussions be conducted in a spirit of good will, keeping in mind that the primary aim of the course is not to address the *presence of difference* within contemporary Christianity, but rather the *absence of depth*. The course is specifically intended for those seeking to deepen their understanding of God by nurturing the *thinking faith that alone is pleasing to Him*. This is not some special faith: it is the faith commanded in Scripture, exhibited by the apostles and other New Testament followers of Christ, and seen in many subsequent generations of Christians. It will require putting on one's thinking cap and putting forth mental effort—the kind of effort Christ sought when He spoke in parables and asked difficult questions.

For more information on C.S. Lewis and background on the actual writing of *Mere Christianity*, I strongly recommend *C.S. Lewis: A Companion and Guide*, by Walter Hooper, 1996, pp. 1-126, 303-328.

Study Formats

Study Format: One Course of 12 Lessons

☐ Lesson 1	Preface, Book 1: Chapters 1& 2	☐ Lesson 7	Book 3: Chapters 7 & 8
☐ Lesson 2	Book 1: Chapters 3, 4 & 5	☐ Lesson 8	Book 3: Chapters 9, 10, 11, 12
☐ Lesson 3	Book 2: Chapters 1 & 2	☐ Lesson 9	Book 4: Chapter 1, 2 & 3
☐ Lesson 4	Book 2: Chapters 3, 4 & 5	☐ Lesson 10	Book 4: Chapter 4, 5 & 6
☐ Lesson 5	Book 3: Chapters 1, 2 & 3	☐ Lesson 11	Book 4: Chapter 7, 8 & 9
☐ Lesson 6	Book 3: Chapters 4, 5 & 6	☐ Lesson 12	Book 4: Chapter 10 & 11

Study Format: Three Courses of 4 Lessons

First Course:

☐ Lesson 1	Preface, Book 1: Chapters 1& 2	Third Course:	
☐ Lesson 2	Book 1: Chapters 3, 4 & 5	☐ Lesson 1	Book 4: Chapter 1, 2 & 3
☐ Lesson 3	Book 2: Chapters 1 & 2	☐ Lesson 2	Book 4: Chapter 4, 5 & 6
☐ Lesson 4	Book 2: Chapters 3, 4 & 5	☐ Lesson 3	Book 4: Chapter 7, 8 & 9
		☐ Lesson 4	Book 4: Chapter 10 & 11

Second Course:

☐ Lesson 1	Book 3: Chapters 1, 2 & 3
☐ Lesson 2	Book 3: Chapters 4, 5 & 6
☐ Lesson 3	Book 3: Chapters 7 & 8
☐ Lesson 4	Book 3: Chapters 9, 10, 11 & 12

Study Format: One Protracted Course of 33 Lessons

☐ Lesson 1	Preface	☐ Lesson 18	Book 3: Chapter 7
☐ Lesson 2	Book 1: Chapter 1	☐ Lesson 19	Book 3: Chapter 8
☐ Lesson 3	Book 1: Chapter 2	☐ Lesson 20	Book 3: Chapter 9
☐ Lesson 4	Book 1: Chapter 3	☐ Lesson 21	Book 3: Chapter 10
☐ Lesson 5	Book 1: Chapter 4	☐ Lesson 22	Book 3: Chapter 11 & 12
☐ Lesson 6	Book 1: Chapter 5	☐ Lesson 23	Book 4: Chapter 1
☐ Lesson 7	Book 2: Chapter 1	☐ Lesson 24	Book 4: Chapter 2
☐ Lesson 8	Book 2: Chapter 2	☐ Lesson 25	Book 4: Chapter 3
☐ Lesson 9	Book 2: Chapter 3	☐ Lesson 26	Book 4: Chapter 4
☐ Lesson 10	Book 2: Chapter 4	☐ Lesson 27	Book 4: Chapter 5
☐ Lesson 11	Book 2: Chapter 5	☐ Lesson 28	Book 4: Chapter 6
☐ Lesson 12	Book 3: Chapter 1	☐ Lesson 29	Book 4: Chapter 7
☐ Lesson 13	Book 3: Chapter 2	☐ Lesson 30	Book 4: Chapter 8
☐ Lesson 14	Book 3: Chapter 3	☐ Lesson 31	Book 4: Chapter 9
☐ Lesson 15	Book 3: Chapter 4	☐ Lesson 32	Book 4: Chapter 10
☐ Lesson 16	Book 3: Chapter 5	☐ Lesson 33	Book 4: Chapter 11
☐ Lesson 17	Book 3: Chapter 6		

INTRODUCTION
WHY A "THINKING" FAI

"But we have the mind of Christ."

1 Cor. 2:16

Remember the old joke that asked, "What do you call someone who graduates at the bottom of the class in medical school?" The answer? "A doctor." But you probably wouldn't ever seek out that doctor to become patient, would you? Similarly, "What do you call someone who walks down a church aisle, makes a profession of faith in Jesus Christ and then never does anything to go on further and higher in their knowledge of Christ, their love for God or their walk in the Spirit?" The answer? "A Christian." And similarly, you probably wouldn't ever seek out that shallow, in-name-only Christian to *be with*—much less *be like*—would you?

Probably not, or you wouldn't have chosen to read this book.

Not long after my own conversion, I was asked by a seasoned church member how I had become a Christian. I told him about an *intrusion* that occurred one day in my life, unsolicited, unexpected and unexplainable. The intrusion was a *sensation* I had never experienced before and which, I truthfully never knew human beings could experience. To make matters more confusing, the sensation returned...and then again and again—well over 200 times I estimated—I told the listener before going on to briefly recount my four year search to understand it.

Being a Psychobiology undergraduate student at the time, I was soon able to dismiss epilepsy, a brain tumor, bipolar disorder or some prankster with drug-dipped darts and began to broaden my enquiry. I took it upon myself to entirely read the major texts of most of the world's foremost religions—including the Bible. I also read a number of histories, biographies and philosophical, psychological and theological works. I became convinced that my experiences were neither uncommon nor limited to any one race or class of people but, for reasons unclear to me, they were simply not spoken about.[1] Then I was introduced to a man who would forever change my life.

This man, of course, was C.S. Lewis and my introduction came through one of his writings, albeit not *Mere Christianity*, but a "suffocatingly subjective" autobiographical cousin, *Surprised By Joy*. In the book, Lewis recounted his early life and thought up to the time, when as a don at as Oxford University, he experienced his own conversion. The man I met in Lewis was one who had, without psychotropic intoxicants or austere, exotic religious practices (both of which were common in the literature of my college days), encountered my same recurring experiences of "Joy"

...e called them), had rationally struggled with many of my own questions, but who, in the end, ...bandoned neither his *experiences* nor his *reason*. It was then that Lewis brought me to a significant realization: if the experiences I was having were not mere random twists of the brain, then they must be purposeful and, as I began to suspect, their purpose was none other than that of *bait*—I had unwittingly been lulled into a trap. For "Joy" was not a sensation of fulfillment and therefore an end in itself.

As Lewis described, "It is difficult to find words strong enough for the sensation which came over me; Milton's 'enormous bliss' of Eden...comes somewhere near it. It was a sensation, of course, of desire; but desire for what?...and before I knew what I desired, the desire itself was gone, the whole glimpse withdrawn, the world turned commonplace again, or only stirred by a longing that had just ceased...[it was an] unsatisfied desire which is itself more desirable than any other satisfaction...[and therefore doubtful that] anyone who has tasted it would ever, if both were in his power, exchange it for all the pleasures in the world."[2] Yes, an intense, enormous, unsatisfied and *desirable* desire, but a desire for what?

When I came to see that merely desiring a desire was not the same as seeking to find and be fulfilled by the desire's object, two things occurred.

First, several hypothetical explanations espousing goals of obtaining some state of mind, like happiness or pleasure, fell away. A practical though crude analogy may be helpful: Imagine a boy, shipwrecked on a deserted island, who begins to go through puberty and start having new desires he has never experienced before—are the desires simply for producing an aroused state of mind or are they for some specific object yet unknown to him? While not meaning to be dismissive, it seemed to me that the overriding objective of many Eastern Religions and certainly all the emerging Western drug philosophies of that time were, therefore, akin to mental masturbation.

Second, if the object of the desire actually existed, what might it be or be like relative to other known human categories of desire? Was it a desire for something like food or drink or new shoes? Or was it a desire for something more, a desire for another living being? The latter produced a problem: could the object I so inconsolably longed for possibly be inconsolably *longing back* for me? I was entering terrain that was no longer safe.

As though I had been asleep, I suddenly awakened to the fact that I had not initiated this quest I was undertaking. Like a fish in pursuit of a smaller fish that unexpectedly sees a larger fish coming after itself from behind, I now found myself as less the predator and more the prey, as less the 'seeker' and more the 'sought.' Frightened yet still longing, as in the early bloom of new love, I knew I was no longer dealing with either the imaginary or innocuous but a living being, real and, apparently, relentless. I found I had entered into intellectual "checkmate"—to again use Lewis's own description—and there was no *honest* way out. I finally conceded, "If something is there, if you are there, show me."

The *possibility* of the existence of a real, living, *desiring* supernatural God continued to haunt me for a few more weeks. Finally one bright snowy day, following neither an invitation nor an alter call, I walked out of a small church in Idaho astonished by the collision of desires that had just taken place and *knowing* Christ was who He claimed to be. *Believing Him had not made Him real; but because He was real and knowable, I believed Him.*

After hearing my account, the man who inquired about my conversion looked at me and incredulously replied, "You mean you did all that when the only thing you had to do was go from your head down to your heart?!"

Two things disturbed him. First, he was of the mindset that it should not have taken me four years to be converted—it could be done in the time it took to get in an elevator on one floor and get out on another. Apparently the lengthy conversions of Augustine, Martin Luther and C.S. Lewis had no place in his view of Christianity.

Second, the journey from one's head to one's heart was a statement about *epistemology* or knowledge or thinking. By it he did not mean "knowledge plus" or a "knowledge that surpasses our human reason." Indeed, for him it meant that *belief was the ability to give up the need to know; faith meant no longer having to think.* In other words, going from your head to your heart meant leaving your head behind, not having both.

I respectfully chose to just smile back at him because, as a young believer, I lacked both the confidence and experience to express what was truly inside me: "Yes, sir, and had I not met with so many superficial clichés like your own, it perhaps wouldn't have taken me four years to come to Christ!" In my subsequent 35 years as a Christian, I have never forgotten that conversation inasmuch as I have been reminded of it time and time again by many other well-meaning but otherwise misinformed Christian men and women.

Inherent in the Biblical notions of faith and grace is a trustworthy transference of merit that is necessary to become right with God: as the insufficiency of one's own efforts is humbly recognized, it gives way to the sufficient efforts of Christ on one's behalf. However, this is not an end but a beginning and a point of paramount confusion. Somehow today *grace* has too often come to be used as a synonym for the *absence of volitional effort* while *faith* has come to be used as a synonym for *mental cruise-control.* "I can't earn my salvation" has given way to "I don't have to do anything about my salvation and spirituality." And, "I can't see God but only believe in Him" has given way to "I don't have to learn or know anything more." But neither of these views is Biblical and therefore neither will foster a growing, confident relationship with God. Many Christian writers—from New Testament times clear up to today—have addressed this: "Faith is not opposed to knowledge; it is opposed to sight. Grace is not opposed to effort; it is opposed to earning." [3]

The paucity of brothers and sisters in Christ who work at thinking through their faith is the 'open secret' of Christianity today. This does not mean a scarcity of Christians with specialized Ph.D.s; it means a scarcity of ordinary lay Christian individuals who understand that their faith must be mentally disciplined beyond merely hearing a weekly sermon or attending a Sunday School class. We have not been left with, "You shall love the Lord your God with all your heart and with all your soul but *with little to none of your mind.*"

The issue is this: because we as Christians have failed to think as our Lord did and as His apostles did and as many succeeding generations of Christians also did, because we have failed to recognize, cultivate and exercise the *mind of Christ* that indwells every Christian, Christianity today is no longer the *thinking faith* it was intended to be. Because we have not *set our minds* as such, we have slipped from the loving path of God's leading, we have become distracted from His call to godliness, and we have failed to progress along His planned transformation from "statues"—as Lewis called us—to *real* sons of God. The result has been devastating. Rather than being distinct within this world due to God's indwelling presence, we have become indistinguishable from it. Rather than being spouses, parents, workers and citizens of honor, prudence, integrity, endurance and courage, we have become superficial, dishonest, lazy, greedy and 'cool'. Rather than being pleasing to our God, I fear we have become a plague.

I wish that these observations were mine alone, but unfortunately they are not; the problem is not endemic but pandemic and has spread throughout today's education, culture (society) and *church*. The resulting affect upon Christianity has been mind numbing. For a clearer picture of this, please refer to **Appendix 1**. We now live in what is probably the most *anti*-intellectual era in the history of Western civilization. By this, I do not mean *non*-intellectual as in a humanity that has somehow *lost* its capacity to think and discern between true and false or real and sham. I mean *anti*-intellectual as in a humanity that has *chosen against* the exercise and use of that capacity. Like someone choosing to close his eyes because he has lost confidence in the existence of *light*, humanity appears to be choosing to close its mind because it has lost confidence in *truth*. The resulting *shallow-thinking* has become the new "norm" in education, culture and the church. Consequently, reason, well-informed character and conviction within Christianity have given way to feelings, fads and infatuations.

Superficial Christians are the product of a superficial Christianity. Superficial Christianity is an inanimate monument with everything carved out in stone that keeps feeding the mind of its adherents *lifeless* life applications. Instead of fostering *living thought* it freezes it. For "If Christians cannot communicate as thinking beings, they are reduced to encountering one another only at the shallow level of gossip and small talk. Hence [today's] modern problem—the loneliness of the thinking Christian." [4]

Deep Christians are *thinking* Christians. They reject all calls to forfeit the cultivation of their minds just because the "Christian mind is too provocative, too dangerous, too revolutionary [and if] nourished, if fed fat on the milk of the word, it would perhaps collide so violently with the secular mind which dominates our comfortable and complacent set-up that we Christians shall find ourselves, mentally at least, persecuted again."[5] Rather, the thinking Christian knows that, "Wherever men think and talk, the banner will have to be raised. Not, of course, for the purpose of pursuing a ceaseless propaganda campaign, but for the purpose of pursuing clarity and integrity. Not that we should convert, but that we should be understood. Not that the Christian mind should become the immediate and overwhelming vehicle of all truth to all men, but that the Christian mind should be recognized for what it is: something different, something distinctive, something with depth, hardness, solidity; a pleasure to fight with and a joy to be beaten by."[6]

Deep-thinking Christians are not the by-product of some *super-Christianity* or *Christianity plus*; they are simply believers transformed by a greater and greater awareness of being possessed with the mind of Christ coupled with a recognition that the mind of Christ is not just off to the side sputtering in some corner. As Lewis put it, "God is no fonder of intellectual slackers than of any other slackers...Anyone who is honestly trying to be a Christian will soon find his intelligence being sharpened: one of the reasons why it needs no special education to be a Christian is that Christianity is an education itself."[7]

What then are we to do? Our options run between "Stay low to keep the status quo" and "Let's get a big bunch of people going on this." Whereas the first of these extremes denies the very power God has placed within us, the latter overinflates that power so as to run ahead and leave God behind, as Israel did at Ai.

The correct, God-ordained option is one of those wonderful, biblical paradoxes. Wherein primarily taking care of oneself goes against our commanded evangelical sensibilities about going into and caring for the world, recall this fact about Paul's evangelism: "The church throughout all Judea and Galilee and Samaria enjoyed peace, being built up; and...it continued to increase" *only after* the brethren had taken the new convert Paul and "sent him away to Tarsus."[8] Indeed Paul had been bringing the gospel to others, but a decade and some years later, he had learned to take enough care of himself to bring others not merely *the gospel*, but *the gospel incarnate*. In later years, he would write to the Corinthians, "I determined to know nothing among you except Jesus Christ, and Him crucified. And I was with you in weakness and in fear and in trembling. And my message and my preaching were not in persuasive words of wisdom, but in demonstration of the Spirit and of power, that your faith should not rest on the wisdom of men, but on the power of God."[9]

The paradoxical best way to love our neighbor is to love them as we love ourselves; and the best way to love ourselves—within God's Spirit, love, grace and will—is to work with what He has enabled us to work with the best—*ourselves*. This means training our minds, disciplining our thinking and *exercising the very mind of Christ within us*. It is *this* mind that knows how deeply it is loved; and it is this mind that knows how deeply it can love others.

The best and most authentic evidence of true Christianity is a Christian; and, unfortunately, the worst evidence is the same. We evangelicals may have sold ourselves a false bill of goods by making our first priority *evangelism* instead of making it what Christ declared it should be. It is precisely at this point that *Mere Christianity* enters the picture. To some, *Mere Christianity* is an appetizer; to others it is an apologetic; and to still others it is an affirmation: but to all, especially at this hour, it should be seen for what it actually is—the acknowledgment of *what Christianity actually is*. "It is quite right," Lewis wrote, "to go away from [the words of the Bible] for a moment in order to make some special point clear. But you must always go back. Naturally God knows how to describe Himself much better than we know how to describe Him."[10]

C.S. Lewis and *Mere Christianity* are not substitutes for Christ and Scripture, but they are, for a moment, enormously helpful in making some special points clear as we transform from being creatures inhabiting a universe haunted by a-right-and-wrong-that-we-fail-to-live-by into being "new men." Subjecting ourselves to reading, thinking about and discussing these points—the way Christ taught and trained His disciples—will, one may trust, serve to bring us not only *back to* but also '*further up and further in*' to Christ and Scripture. Put differently, thinking with the mind of Christ will make us think more like Christ and thinking more like Christ will make us more Christ-like: "This is the whole of Christianity...the Church exists for nothing else but to draw men into Christ, to make them little Christs. If they are not doing that, all the cathedrals, clergy, missions, even the Bible itself, are simply a waste of time. God became Man for no other purpose. It is even doubtful, you know, whether the whole universe was created for any other purpose."[11]

PREFACE

Lewis begins by stating he is not offering help to anyone hesitating between two denominations or overly concerned about certain disputed matters. His objective is "the defense of what [Richard] Baxter called 'mere' Christianity."

1. Where would you place yourself on the "denomination" chart below? Horizontally, do you lean more toward the Frozen Chosen or the Hurried Worried? Vertically, do you lean more to the Surgical Liturgicals or the Holly Rollies? Mark an 'X' where you would locate your beliefs:

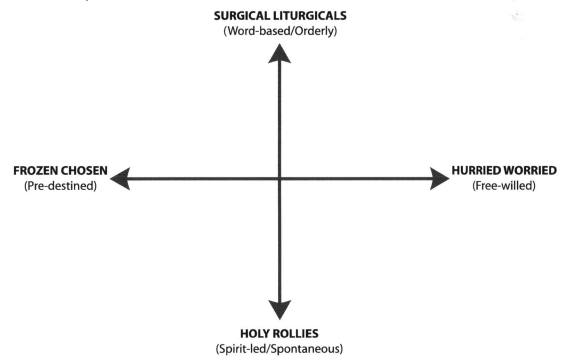

2. In *your opinion*, what benefits do you think are obtained from denominations?

3. In *your opinion*, what detriments do you think come from denominations?

4. What does Lewis mean by a Christianity that is 'mere'? (para. 8)

5. How does Lewis use the word "gentleman" to clarify the meaning of "Christian"? (para. 10-13)

6. For "extra-credit" and the "extra-curious", who was Richard Baxter?

Answer Guide available at www.MereChristianity.org

Discussion Notes

Book 1
Right and Wrong as a Clue to the Meaning of the Universe

Chapter 1: The Law of Human Nature

1.   What is it that we can learn from people disagreeing or quarreling? (para. 1-2)

2.   What are some of the different names Lewis says this can or has been called? (para. 3)

3.   How is the Law of Human Nature different from other laws of nature? (para. 3-4)

4.   Why in the past have people called this Rule about Right and Wrong the Law of Nature? (para. 5)

5.   On what basis have some denied that the Law of (Human) Nature is known to all men? (para. 6)

6.   How does Lewis respond to this denial? (para. 7-8)

7.   Agreeing that Right and Wrong are *real or objective* and not merely a matter of taste, preference or opinion, what is the next point Lewis makes about our human Law of Nature? (para. 9-10)

8.   Put Lewis's final summary into your own words: (para. 11)

Answer Guide available at www.MereChristianity.org

Discussion Notes

Chapter 2: Some Objections

1.   **First objection:** Isn't the Moral Law or Law of Human Nature just an innate or inbred herd instinct?

A.   What are some "herd instincts" that Lewis notes? (para. 2)

B.   How is the Moral Law perceived or felt differently than an instinct, desire or impulse? (para. 2)

C.   Using music as an analogy, how does Lewis distinguish the Moral Law from an instinct? (para. 2)

D.   Another way to make this distinction is by supposing we had two opposing instincts but no inner Moral Law: what would determine which instinct would be followed? (para. 3)

F. Why can't there be one impulse which is always good that is actually the Moral Law? (para. 4,5)

2. **Second objection:** Isn't the Moral Law simply a social convention, learned by education?
    A. List some human conventions you have learned from your parents or society:

    B. What example of a real truth (which exists whether or not it was ever taught) does Lewis cite? (para. 6)

    C. What two reasons does Lewis give for the Moral Law being a reality and not a convention? (para. 7)

    D. What is Lewis's reply to the argument that Moral Law was responsible for witch burning in the past? (para. 8)

Answer Guide available at www.MereChristianity.org

Discussion Notes

Chapter 3: The Reality of the Law

1. In review, what are the "two odd things about the human race"? (para. 1)

2. One may say that breaking the Moral Law of Right and Wrong only points out that people are not perfect and ask why one would want to do that. How does Lewis respond? (para. 1)

3. The notion of something being *imperfect* or *not being what it 'ought' to be* raises a significant point. Lewis clarifies this point by looking more closely at the laws of nature. How does he differentiate between the Laws of Nature as applied to stones or trees and the Law of Human Nature? (para. 1-3)

4. One might be tempted to try to explain away this oddity of the Law of Human Nature by saying it is really only some feature of the Laws of Nature that happens to be inconvenient or non-beneficial to oneself. Why is this not true? (para. 4)

5.   Others might try to explain away the Law of Human Nature in terms of benefiting society or humanity as a whole. How does this fall short? (para. 5)

6.   *Thinking Cap Question:* What do the above notions of *blaming others for not being perfect, personal beneficence* and *societal beneficence* each have in common relative to the Law of Human Nature?

Answer Guide available at www.MereChristianity.org

At the end of this chapter, Lewis writes, "Consequently, this Rule of Right and Wrong, or Law of Human Nature, or whatever you call it, must somehow or other be a real thing—a thing that is really there, not made up by ourselves." Rhetorically ask yourself, "Do I actually believe that *right and wrong* universally and inescapably possess or haunt all human beings around the world?" To help you formulate an answer, read through **Appendix 2** which is taken from C.S. Lewis's *The Abolition of Man*.

Discussion Notes

Chapter 4: What Lies Behind The Law

The *Laws of Nature* are 'facts of' or 'a part of' of nature itself. Saying that these Laws govern nature is really just another way of saying what in fact nature does. The *Law of Human Nature* then must be something different, something above and beyond the actual facts of what humans do. Lewis now turns to see what this tells us about the universe we live in.

1. Throughout history, people have wondered what the universe is and how it came about. Essentially <u>three</u> different views have been held (the third view comes at the end of the chapter). What is the first view and what does it embrace as true? (para. 2)

2. What is the second view and what does it regard as true? (para. 2)

3. Some (biased?) modern views often say that human knowledge has progressed from the theological to the philosophical to the scientific and that the best explainers of the universe today are no longer clergymen or philosophers but scientists. But what exactly can scientists tell us? (para. 2)

4. What other "one thing, and only one, in the whole universe [do] we know more about than what we could ever learn from external (scientific) observation"? How do we know it? (para. 3)

5.   In your own words, contrast the "Materialist/Scientific" view via the architect-as-a-wall analogy with the "Religious/Human Being" view via the mailman-with-little-paper-packets analogy. (para. 4)

6.   What is the third view (not mentioned during the radio broadcasts) and what does it put forward as true? (para. 6)

Answer Guide available at www.MereChristianity.org

Discussion Notes

Chapter 5: We Have Cause To Be Uneasy

So the Law of Human Nature is like someone or something trying to send us letters from outside the material universe. This sounds like a trick or religion wrapped up in philosophy and logic; and, if it only turns out to be religion, that has been tried and you cannot turn the clock back. Lewis replies to this with three points:

1.   What is his first point about putting the clock back? (para. 2)

2.   Regarding his second point, "religious jaw:"
        A.   Where so far are we getting our knowledge? (para. 3)

        B.   What two bits of evidence do we have available? (para. 3)

        C.   What can we expect if the universe is not governed by an absolute goodness? (para. 3)

D.   What can we expect if the universe is governed by an absolute goodness? (para. 3)

3.   What is his third point about the roundabout manner he chose to get to his real subject? (para. 4)

Answer Guide available at www.MereChristianity.org

Discussion Notes

BOOK 2
WHAT CHRISTIANS BELIEVE

Chapter 1: The Rival Conceptions of God

1.   What is one thing that Christians do *not* need to believe but atheists do? (para. 1)

2.   The first big division in humanity separates a majority of people who believe in some sort of God or gods from a minority who do not. List the members of the two groups that Lewis notes. (para. 2)

<u>Non-believers in a God or gods:</u>   <u>Believers in a God or gods:</u>

3.   The next big division separates those with a God-belief by the sort of God they believe in. One view is called "Pantheism" and the other "Theism." Characterize the difference between these two views of God: 1.) **Ethically** in terms of good and evil; 2.) **Cosmologically** in terms of how God is related to the universe; and 3.) **Sociologically** in terms of which groups or individuals adhere to the views. (para. 3,4)

View of God	Pantheism	Theism
Ethical or Moral Perspective		
Cosmological Perspective		
Adherent Groups or Individuals		

4.   What big question is raised if God is good? Before his conversion, how did Lewis respond to Christian answers to this question? (para. 5)

5.   What did Lewis finally come to see about his argument against the existence of God (recall the 'ought')? (para. 6)

Answer Guide available at www.MereChristianity.org

Discussion Notes

Chapter 2: The Invasion

1.   Like atheism, what other view does CLS say is too simple to explain the universe and the 'ought' within us? (para. 1) Look up (or Google) the word "Deism" and write out a definition.

2.   Why is it no good to ask for a simple religion and in what two ways do anti-Christians use "simplicity" to attack Christianity? (para. 2,3)

3.   What then, according to Lewis, is the appeal of Christianity as an explanation? (para. 4,5)

4.   What is the problem, restated by Lewis, and what are the "only two views that face all the facts"? (para. 6)

5.   Define "Dualism" and note some of the reasons why it fails as an explanation. (para. 7-9)

6.   How are the Christian and Dualism explanations of the badness or evil-in-the-universe similar and how are they different? (para. 10,11)

7.   Using a war analogy, how then does Lewis describe Christianity? (para. 12)

See **Appendix 3** for a summary of the rival concepts of God.

Answer Guide available at www.MereChristianity.org

Discussion Notes

Chapter 3: The Shocking Alternative

1. The Prince of this World is evil, but a good God is in charge. How did this happen? (para. 1-4)

2. What point about free will does Lewis make concerning a cow, dog, child, ordinary man, and a superhuman spirit? (para. 5)

3. How did Satan's deception to 'be like gods' become what Lewis calls "the key to history"? (para. 6,7)

4. What three things did God do to prepare humanity for His solution to Satan's plot? (para. 8)

    1.

    2.

3.

5.   What then is God's shocking alternative solution? Comment on His being a Jew, His forgiving sins and His claims about being humble. (para. 9-11)

6.   Based on what Jesus says of Himself we are not given the option of calling Him a great moral teacher. What "tri-lemma" then is left? (para. 12)

Answer Guide available at gwww.MereChristianity.or

To go deeper into what God did to prepare humanity refer again to **Appendix 2** (conscience-sense of right and wrong) and **Appendix 4** ("good dreams" sent to the human race and preparation of the Jews).

Discussion Notes

Chapter 4: The Perfect Penitent

1. God has landed in our enemy-occupied world to teach us, of course, but about what? (para. 1,2)

2. In Lewis's discussion of Christ's death, what points do you think are important? (para. 3-5)

3. Lewis says that "being let off" or "footing the bill" may be too simple a theory of what Christ has done for *fallen man*. Why? (para. 6,7)

4. The process of surrender or repentance is a "kind of death" or "killing part of yourself." What is meant by "only a bad person needs to repent: only a good person can repent perfectly"? (para. 7,8)

5. How does God becoming a man help to resolve this problem? (para. 9)

6.   What response does Lewis give to those who complain that Christ's suffering and death were easier because He was both God and Man? (para. 10)

Answer Guide available at www.MereChristianity.org

Discussion Notes

Chapter 5: The Practical Conclusion

1. Christ's perfect surrender and humiliation as God-Man brought about what kind of change for mankind? (para. 1)

2. What are *your* thoughts on the three ways the new Christ-life is spread to us? (para. 2-4)

3. According to Lewis what significance do our own efforts have to "copy Christ"? (para. 5-7)

4. Do you agree with Lewis (in para. 8) about God's "arrangements about other people" with regard to salvation and His new life?

5. If the spread of God's new life is so important, why does God's invasion still remain so disguised and secret? (para. 9)

6. Extra credit question: At the beginning of this chapter and elsewhere in *Mere Christianity*, Lewis alludes to evolution. Do you think he is advocating evolution? **(see Appendix 5)**

Answer Guide available at www.MereChristianity.org

Discussion Notes

BOOK 3
CHRISTIAN BEHAVIOR

Chapter 1: The Three Parts of Morality

In many people's minds, <u>morality</u> often means something that interferes with or stops a good time. In reality, "moral rules are directions for running the human machine" to prevent strains, frictions, and breakdowns. At first, when we are learning to use our human machines, the rules may go against our natural inclinations. However in the long run, every moral failure will cause future problems. Therefore, by talking about rules and obedience instead of preferential 'ideals' or 'idealism,' we will better remind ourselves of what is at stake.

1.   Use the fleet of ships and the band analogies to explain the two ways the human machine goes wrong. (para. 3)

2.   Using these same above analogies, explain a third thing that needs to be taken into account about the human machine? (para. 4)

3.   Sum up, then, in your own words, the three parts of morality. (para. 5)
        1.

2.

3.

4. Which of these three parts do most modern people usually acknowledge and not disagree much about and why? (para. 6)

5. Why is the second part also important? (para. 6,7)

6. List some of the reasons Lewis sites for the third part of morality also being important. (para. 8,9)

7. Thinking cap question: what are the biblical names for these three parts of morality?

Answer Guide available at www.MereChristianity.org

Discussion Notes

Chapter 2: The 'Cardinal Virtues'

This chapter was not originally broadcast over the air because of time but was added later to the book. Instead of three parts, Lewis divides morality the way older writers did into seven parts or 'virtues.' Four of them—Prudence, Temperance, Justice and Fortitude—are called "Cardinal" (or "Pivotal") virtues; the other three—Charity, Hope, and Faith—are called "Theological" virtues and will be discussed in later chapters.

1.   What is PRUDENCE and why do many Christians today fail to practice it? (para. 4)

2.   TEMPERANCE today is equated with "teetotalism," but what did it originally mean? (para. 5,6)

3.   Beyond what goes on in law courts, what does JUSTICE also consist of? (para. 7)

4.   What does FORTITUDE include? (para. 7)

5.   Lewis makes a distinction between a person doing some virtuous act and a person who is virtuous. What three reasons does he give as to why this distinction is important? (para. 8,9)

1.

2.

3.

6.   Thinking cap question: what are more common biblical names for the "cardinal virtues"?
Prudence =

Temperance =

Justice =

Fortitude =

Answer Guide available at www.MereChristianity.org

Discussion Notes

Chapter 3: Social Morality

1. What is the 'first thing to get clear' about Christ and Christian social morality? (para. 1)

2. What is the 'second thing to get clear' about a Christian social morality for our world? (para. 2)

3. What are the right and the wrong ways 'the Church ought to give us a lead' to make society better? (para. 3)

4. Lewis says the New Testament hints at what a fully Christian society would look like: a 'Leftist, obedient, and cheerful' society. (para. 4,5) Why would or wouldn't you want to live in a society like this?

5. Heathen Greeks, Old Testament Jews, and Christians of the Middle Ages were all against a one kind of economic system. (para. 6) What is the system, and what are its pros and cons today?

6.   Whether we 'give a man a fish' or 'give a man a fishing pole and teach him to fish,' giving or charity remains one of our moral duties today as Christians. What does Lewis say is "the only safe rule" for giving and what, for many of us, is the great obstacle? (para. 7) Please see **Appendix 6**.

7.   What probably is the real snag most of us run up against in drawing up blueprints for a Christian society? (para. 8) Please see **Appendix 7**.

Answer Guide available at www.MereChristianity.org

Discussion Notes

Chapter 4: Morality and Psychoanalysis

We will never get a Christian society unless most of us become Christian individuals. We should not stop working on society to work on ourselves, but we should do both jobs at once. Lewis now wants to look at what the Christian idea of a good man is by first making two general points: **First,** because Christian morality claims to be a technique for putting the human machine right, we should understand how it is related to psychoanalysis which claims to do the same (para. 1-7). **Second,** because Christian morality is often viewed as bargaining with God by keeping a lot of rules, a more accurate view is given (para. 8-10).

1.   When a man makes a moral choice, what two things are involved? What "two kinds" of the second thing are there? (para. 4)

2.   Use the example of the three men going to war (para. 5) to fill in the chart below:

Raw Material of the Men	Result of Psychoanalysis	Result of Moral Effort/Choices
#1 Man with a natural fear of danger	No psychoanalysis needed	
#2 Man with an irrational fear of danger		
#3 Man with an irrational fear of danger		

3.   In view of a person's raw psychological material, why are Christians told not to judge? (para. 6)

4.   Where does most of a man's raw psychological material reside and what will happen after he dies? (para. 7)

5.   Rather than bargaining with God by keeping a lot of rules, how does Lewis view the process of Christian morality? (para. 8, 9) (Does this view agree with Romans 8:5-8?)

6.   Beyond peace, what does Lewis say one obtains when moral choices are moving them in the right direction? (para. 10) (Does this agree with Proverbs 4:18-19?) See **Appendix 8** for more on this.

Answer Guide available at www.MereChristianity.org

Discussion Notes

Chapter 5: Sexual Morality

1.   Christian morality regarding sex is called "chastity." How does the rule of chastity differ from the rule of propriety or modesty? (para. 1)

2.   Chastity is the most unpopular of the Christian virtues or morals. Consequently, it is often concluded that either something is wrong with Christianity or something is wrong with our sexual instinct. Lewis says the problem is with our sexual instinct: what three reasons does he give? (para. 2-6)

    1.   Biological purpose (para. 3) —

    2.   Strip-tease and starvation (para. 4,5) —

    3.   Perversion and propaganda (para. 6) —

3.   What three positive points about Christianity and sex does Lewis make? (para. 7)
    1.   Old Christian writers (para. 7) —

    2.   View of the body (para. 7) —

    3.   Marriage and love poems (para. 7) —

4.   The "warped" organisms we have inherited from our ancestors are the constant targets of "propaganda in favour of unchastity." Why? (para. 8)

5.   Three reasons are given why it is difficult to desire—much less achieve—complete chastity. What responses does Lewis give for each? (para. 9-13)
    1.   'It's natural' (para. 10) —

2.   'It's impossible' (para. 11,12) —

3.   'It's repression' (para. 13) —

6.   What is Lewis's final point about sex, sins of the flesh and the "centre of Christian" morality? (para. 14)

Answer Guide available at www.MereChristianity.org

Discussion Notes

Chapter 6: Christian Marriage

1. Christian morality about marriage is based on what, meant to combine whom, and intended for what duration? (para. 2,3)

2. Different denominations have different views about allowing divorce, but what do they all regard divorce as? (para. 3)

3. Marriage vows are promises. If people do not believe in permanent marriage, why does Lewis say it is perhaps better for them to live together unmarried? (para. 4-6)

4. Passions lead to promises. But passions are short lived whereas promises are not. What are some good reasons why two people should stay together even when passion has faded? (para. 7-9)

5.   Apart from what novels and films tell us about "being in love," what point is Lewis trying to get across about Christ saying "a thing will not really live until it first dies"? (para. 10-13)

6.   Beyond the Christian idea of the permanence of marriage there is one further and even more unpopular doctrine: *submission!* How does Lewis explain the need for "a head" and, if a head, why a man? Do you agree with him? (para. 15)

Answer Guide available at www.MereChristianity.org

Discussion Notes

Chapter 7: Forgiveness

1. On second thought, Lewis suspects that Forgiveness or Loving Thy Enemy or the Christian virtue of Charity may be even more unpopular than the virtue of Chastity. Forgiveness is a 'lovely idea' until we actually have something to forgive; it can become not merely difficult but detestable as in the case of a Pole or a Jew forgiving the Gestapo. Whether or not we think we <u>can</u> forgive, Christianity mandates that we <u>must</u> forgive. What specifically is the mandate? (para. 3)

2. What two things does Lewis suggest trying in order to make forgiving easier? (para. 4)
   1.

   2.

3. List some of the things that 'loving your neighbor as yourself' does not mean? (para. 5)
   1.

2.

3.

4. The real test: what results from incorrectly thinking your enemies to be as bad as possible? (para. 7)

5. On the other hand, does loving your enemy mean not punishing him? (para. 8)

6. If one is allowed to condemn an enemy's acts, punish him and kill him, one may question: 'What is the difference between Christian morality and the ordinary view?' How does Lewis reply? (para. 10,11)

7.

Answer Guide available at www.MereChristianity.org

Discussion Notes

Chapter 8: The Great Sin

1. Christian morality differs most sharply from all other moralities on one particular vice: it is a vice from which no one in the world is free; it is a vice that all people loathe when they see it in others; it is a vice that is rarely acknowledged—except by Christians—inside themselves. The vice is Pride or Self-Conceit. According to Christian teachers, what are some of the characteristics of pride that differentiate it from other vices? (para. 2)

2. "The more pride one had the more one disliked pride in others." What other point about pride causes this and how does it influence other vices such as greed? (para. 3,4)

3. Pride is the chief cause of misery in the world. Unlike other vices which may bring people together, pride always means enmity between man and man, and man and God. How are pride and knowing God related? (para. 5-7)

4. How does the devil deceptively use the spiritual vice of pride against the vices of our animal natures? (para. 8)

5.   List/briefly explain four possible misconceptions about pride that Lewis states should be guarded against. (para. 9-13)

1. (para. 10)

2. (para. 11)

3. (para. 12)

4. (para. 13)

Answer Guide available at www.MereChristianity.org

Discussion Notes

Chapter 9: Charity

The four "Cardinal" virtues are *Prudence, Temperance, Justice* and *Fortitude*. We will now look at the three "Theological" virtues of *Charity, Hope* and *Faith*. This chapter deals with Charity. Charity means Forgiveness (discussed in Chapter 7). But it also has another meaning.

1.   Following "Sexual Morality," Lewis discussed "Christian Marriage." Now following "The Great Sin" (or *Pride*), Lewis chose to discuss 'Charity.' Thinking cap question: what was his likely reason for doing this?

2.   What has the word "Charity" come to mean today? (para. 2)

3.   But what wider meaning did Charity originally have? (para. 2)

4.   According to Lewis, what doesn't and does 'Love, in the Christian sense' mean? (para. 3)

5. What doesn't and does this state of will or love for ourselves and our neighbors mean? (para. 4)

6. How can our affections affect our Charity and what is the one simple rule for us all to use? (para. 5)

7. In terms of Charity and affection, what is difference between a Christian and a worldly man? (para. 6-8)

8. How does this all apply to our love for God? (para. 9,10)

Answer Guide available at www.MereChristianity.org

Discussion Notes

Chapter 10: Hope

Hope is the next of the "Theological" virtues Lewis addresses.

1.   What does Lewis say Hope is? (para. 1)

2.   What does Lewis say Hope isn't? (para. 1)

3.   How then is Hope for the eternal world connected or related to our present world? (para. 1)

4.   What are the two reasons many of us find it difficult "to want Heaven"? (para. 2) For more on this, see **Appendix 9**.

5.   Regarding the second reason—failing to recognize our real longings for Heaven and substituting them with other objects that can never satisfy—Lewis lists three ways we can deal with this, two wrong ways and one right. Briefly explain the three ways. (para. 3-5)
        1.   The Fool's Way (para. 3)

2.   The Way of the Disillusioned 'Sensible Man' (para. 4)

3.   The Christian Way (para. 5)

6.   What rejoinder does Lewis offer for facetious people who say hoping for Heaven is ridiculous because they do not want "to spend eternity playing harps"? (para. 6)

Answer Guide available at www.MereChristianity.org

Discussion Notes

Chapter 11: Faith

The final "Theological" virtue is faith. Christians use the word Faith in two senses:

1.   The **first** sense simply means Belief—accepting or regarding as true the doctrines of Christianity. But Faith in this sense is also considered to be a virtue—why did this used to puzzle Lewis? (para. 1)

2.   What did Lewis come to understand that allowed him to see Faith as a virtue? What are some of his illustrating examples (para. 2,3)
      1.

      2.

      3.

3.   Rephrase what the sense of Faith isn't and what it is (para. 4-6):
      Faith is not (para. 4):

Faith is (para. 5,6):

4. Faith in the **second**, higher sense is more difficult. After the recognition of a shortcoming —for example, pride—the next step should be some serious attempt to practice Christian virtues. What is the main thing we learn from doing this and consequently what do we come to see about Christ? (para. 7)

5. What two discovery results has God been waiting for you to realize? (para. 8,9)
    1. (para. 8)

    2. (para.9)

At this point, I recommend carefully reading through **Appendix 10**.

Answer Guide available at www.MereChristianity.org

Discussion Notes

Chapter 12: Faith

Chapter 12 continues on about Faith in the **second**, higher sense. Lewis starts by saying that if this chapter doesn't mean anything to you, then just drop it. If the previous chapter and Appendix 10 did not assist in understanding our transition from the 'ought' to 'practicing the virtues,' then come back to this chapter at another time. There are a "great many things that cannot be understood until after you have gone a certain distance along the Christian road."

Explain what Lewis is seeking to clarify in the following five statements:

1. "I mean really discovered" (para. 4)

2. "Do not, I implore you, start asking yourselves, 'Have I reached that moment?'" (para. 5)

3. "I know the words 'leave it to God' can be misunderstood." (para. 6)

4. "Christians have often disputed as to whether what leads the Christian home is good actions or Faith in Christ." (para. 7)

5. "Though Christianity seems at the first to be all about morality, all about duty and rule and guilt and virtue, yet it leads you on, out of all that, into something beyond." (para. 8)

Answer Guide available at www.MereChristianity.org

Discussion Notes

BOOK 4
BEYOND PERSONALITY: FIRST STEPS IN THE DOCTRINE OF THE TRINITY

Chapter 1: Making and Begetting

1. Some advise a plain 'practical religion' (simple dos and don'ts) while others recommend a personal 'vague religion' (feeling God in nature and such). Against their advice, Lewis advocates 'Theology' because he does not believe the ordinary person is a fool or child. Theology is the science (or study) of God; and those who want to think about God want the clearest and most accurate ideas about Him. How then is Theology like a map? (para. 4,5)

2. Theology is practical. Without it there is not the absence of any ideas about God but the presence of wrong ones. Theology helps us to discern between worked-out-thought-through-REAL-Christianity and so-called-POPULAR-Christianity. What was the popular view of Christ and Christianity in England when *Mere Christianity* was written? (para. 6,7)

3. Real Christianity differs from popular religion. It contains difficult statements like 'Christ is the Son of God' and those who give their confidence to Him can also become 'sons of

God.' Our becoming sons of God brings us to the center of Theology: Christ is the Son of God 'begotten, not created.' Distinguish between 'begetting' and 'making': (para. 8-13)

Begetting	Making
To beget is to become the of	To create is to
Begetting produces something of the kind	Making produces something of a kind
A man begets	A man makes
God begets	God makes

4.   God *makes* what is not God and that is why men are not Sons of God in the sense that Christ is. Nevertheless everything God has made has some likeness to Himself. Note how God's likeness varies in the different things He has made: (para. 14)

What God Has Made	How It Is "Like" God
Space	
Matter	
Vegetables	
Animals	
Higher Mammals	
Man	

5.   But "natural" man does not possess "Spiritual" life. How are *Bios* and *Zoë* different? (para. 15,16)

Answer Guide available at www.MereChristianity.org

Discussion Notes

Chapter 2: The Three-Personal God

1. So what God the Father begets is God—something of the same kind—like a human father begetting a human son. But Lewis wants to explain another point about God by looking at the belief "that the mysterious something which is behind all other things must be more than a person...a being that is beyond personality." There are two prevailing views: God is *impersonal* or God is ***super-personal***. What is the difference between the views and what bearing does it ultimately have upon human souls becoming united with God? (para. 1-3)

    1.   Impersonal:

    2.   Super-personal:

2. The whole purpose we exist is to be taken into the life of God. Wrong ideas about that life will make it harder. How does Lewis's 3-D discussion apply to our understanding of our 3-P God? (para. 4-7)

3. How can a mere prayer draw us into the life of the Three-Personal God? (para. 8-10)

4. Working through ideas such as 'a God who begets God', a 'God who is Three-Personal' and a 'God who draws us into His life by common acts like prayer' *is* Theology. "Theology is, in a sense, an experimental science...like other experimental sciences in some ways, but not in all." Fill in the chart below to better understand what Lewis is talking about here (guesses are OK): (para. 11-13)

EXPERIMENTAL SCIENCE	% INITIATIVE BY SUBJECT	% INITIATIVE BY YOU
Geology: the study of rocks	by rocks =	by you =
Zoology: the study of animals	by animals =	by you =
Sociology: the study of humans	by other humans =	by you =
Theology: the study of God	by God =	by you =

5. To who does and does not God show Himself? (para. 14-17)

Answer Guide available at www.MereChristianity.org

Discussion Notes

Chapter 3: Time and Beyond

God only begets God. God is One Being but Three distinct Persons. Knowing God rests in God's hands (but *not* knowing Him in ours). Now that we have these concepts under our belt, let's move on to some difficult stuff! **If you like, it is OK to skip this chapter but it may help with some of the difficulties encountered in our own Christian life.**

1. "I believe in God all right, but what I cannot swallow is the idea of Him attending to several hundred million human beings who are all addressing Him at the same moment." How does Lewis respond to this comment? (para. 2-5)

2. Explain how the idea of writing a novel about a character named Mary may be used to better understand God and time. (para. 6-9)

3. How could Christ at the same time be God who knows everything and also a man asking His disciples 'Who touched Me?' (para. 10)

4. Does God's omniscience interfere with our being free-willed beings? (para. 11,12)

Answer Guide available at www.MereChristianity.org

Discussion Notes

Chapter 4: Good Infection

1. The position of 'Book B' above the table is the *result* of 'Book A' that is underneath it. God the Son is the *result* of being *begotten* by God the Father. But the *cause* in each case —'Book A' or God the Father—*did not come before the respective result*. Please explain. (para. 1-4)

2. People's use of 'God is love' is meaningless unless God is what? What does Lewis *reverently* say that Christians mean by 'God is love'? (para. 5,6)

3. What Third *Person* grows out of the love-dance-joint-life of the Father and the Son and what does it all matter? (para. 6-8)

4. How is it possible for us to be taken into the three-Personal life (i.e. to get the 'good infection')? (para. 8,9) Note: Lewis gives a great and concise summary here of what it means to be a Christian.

5.   For extra credit & fun: read Genesis 1 and answer:

    1.   Which one came first, the heavens or the earth?

    2.   Why is day two of creation the only day *not* to receive the commendation, "and God saw that it was good"?

    3.   In the creation account, why is the word "created" (Hebrew, כפא or bara)—seen in the creation of the heavens and the earth (Gen. 1:1), the creation of animal life (Gen. 1:21), and the creation of man (Gen 1: 27)—used only three times?

Answer Guide available at www.MereChristianity.org

Discussion Notes

Chapter 5: The Obstinate Toy Soldiers

1.   At present, two different and opposing kinds of life are at work in us. Describe some of the attributes of the *Bios* or 'natural life'. (para. 2)

2.   Changing our "natural life" into "begotten life" is likened to the difficulty of changing an *obstinate* toy tin soldier into a real little man. What does Lewis say God did to bring about this change in man? (para. 3-5)

3.   So in Christ, 'one tin soldier has come fully and splendidly alive'; yet not just one man but the 'whole human mass' has been affected. How does Lewis (weirdly) explain this? (para. 6,7)

4.   What, then, is the difference He has made to the whole human mass? (para. 8)

Answer Guide available at www.MereChristianity.org

Discussion Notes

Chapter 6: Two Notes

Two notes are added here to avoid two misunderstandings about Chapter 5:

1. **Misunderstanding #1** If God wanted sons instead of 'toy soldiers,' why did He not beget many sons at the onset instead of first making toy soldiers and then painfully transform them into sons? Lewis says there are two parts to the answer to this question, one easy and one difficult. What is the easy part? (para. 2)

2. The second or difficult part of the answer to the question itself has two parts:
   1. All Christians agree there is, in the full and original sense, only one 'Son of God' but could there have been many? Why does Lewis find applying the words 'Could have been' to God nonsensical? (para. 2)

   2. What does Lewis find difficult "about the very idea of the Father begetting many sons from all eternity"? (para. 2)

3. **Misunderstanding #2** The notion that the whole human race is one huge organism, like a tree, should not be confused with the idea that individual difference in people do not matter and are somehow less important than collective things like classes or race. How

does Lewis respond and, in particular, what does he say about the devil's "pairs of opposites"? (para. 3,4)

Answer Guide available at www.MereChristianity.org

Discussion Notes

Chapter 7: Let's Pretend

1. In *Beauty and the Beast* the girl kissed the monster as if it were a man: it turned into a real man. In another story a man had to wear a mask that made him look nicer than he was: eventually his face grew to fit the mask. Up to this point our discussion has been about what God is and does, but what difference does all this Theology make? The difference comes when we put it into practice. What happens when we pray, *Our Father*, why is it a "piece of outrageous cheek", and oddly why should we continue to do it? (para. 1,2)

2. There is a bad kind as well as a good kind of pretense. The good kind moves toward becoming less of a pretense and more of a reality. In "dressing up as Christ", how is our pretense being turned into reality? (para. 3-6)

3. Some may say "I've never had the sense of being helped by an invisible Christ." But Christ works in many ways other than invisibly being at your side. List some that Lewis mentions. (para. 7-9)

4. The New Testament speaks of "being born again", "putting on Christ", Christ "being formed in us" and coming to "have the mind of Christ". What are we to do with these kinds of sayings? (para. 10,11)

5.   As the Christ-life changes us, what two discoveries do we make? (para. 12,13)

    1.   (para. 12)

    2.   (para. 13)

Answer Guide available at www.MereChristianity.org

Discussion Notes

Chapter 8: Is Christianity Hard or Easy?

1. "Dressing up" as a son of God *to become* a son of God is not some special exercise for only the top few. It is "the whole of Christianity." Christianity offers nothing else! With this said, ordinary ideas of "morality" or "being good" therefore differ from Christianity—how so? (para. 1-2)

2. For the one who practices "ordinary morality," one of two likely results will follow—what are they? (para. 3)
    1.

    2.

3. How is the Christian way both harder and easier? (para. 4-6)

4. What is the "real problem of the Christian life", when does it occur, how are we to respond, and what results as we properly respond? (para. 7,8)

5.   I once read the weekly newsletter from a large evangelical church. I counted over 40 different announced activities. What saddened me was that only two appeared to focus upon what is "the whole of Christianity." Per Lewis, how it is easy for the church to get muddled about this and what is the only reason for the church to exist? (para. 9-11)

Answer Guide available at www.MereChristianity.org

Discussion Notes

Chapter 9: Counting the Cost

1. "Be ye perfect"—what does not and what does this mean? (Explain the latter via the "dentist") (para. 1-3)

2. When Christ tells us to "count the cost" what in fact is He warning us of? (para. 4)

3. "God is easy to please, but hard to satisfy" (George McDonald) means He is pleased with even our feeble, stumbling efforts but not content to leave us there. What—even if we never wanted or asked for it—is He changing us into and what "fatal" mistake must we avoid? (para. 5-8)

4. Why must we not be surprised if we are in for a rough time? (para. 9)

5. We are not called to "easy," we are called to "it will be worth it." How does Lewis point this out using Christ's command to *Be ye perfect*? (para. 10)

Answer Guide available at www.MereChristianity.org

Discussion Notes

Chapter 10: Nice People or New Men

This chapter addresses the question, "If Christianity is true why are not all Christians obviously nicer than all non-Christians?" Let's go through it with a lot of short-answer questions:

1.   If conversion to Christianity makes no improvement in actions, the conversion is what? (para. 2)

2.   When we Christians behave badly or fail to behave well, what do we do to Christianity? (para. 2)

3.   Detractors illogically demand post-conversion improvement by "neatly" doing what? (para. 3)

4.   Mass comparisons fail—what is needed to compare the bad Christian and the good Atheist? (para. 4)

5. True or False: Christian Miss Bates should stop telling non-Christian Dick Firkin to "Go to h_ _ _"; conversely Dick should seek to avoid ending up there [*Urban paraphrase*]. (para. 5)

6. Dick Firkin's niceness may cause him not to seek God, but what is the source of his niceness? (para. 6-10)

7. True or False: It may be easier for those who are "poor" in niceness (i.e. mean and nasty) than those who are "rich" in niceness to enter the Kingdom. (para. 11-15)

8. Redemption is not mere improvement—it is not teaching a horse to jump better but what? (para. 16)

9. Once one begins to see that Christianity is probable and then sets up some stupid and unsatisfactory Christian as an example of the boasted new man, what is that person doing? (para. 17)

Answer Guide available at www.MereChristianity.org

Discussion Notes

Chapter 11:The New Men

In this final chapter Lewis discusses two ways in which "New Men" might come into existence. The **first way** is the modern man's way of Darwinian Evolution—through mutations via cosmic rays being filtered by Natural Selection—and the eventual production of the Next Step or what imaginative writers call the "Superman." We will not bother with that way (again, see **Appendix 5** for review).

The **second way** is the Christian view. It sees that the Next Step or New Men have already appeared. But this change is not Evolution because it has not risen from a "natural process" but form something coming into nature from outside. Lewis lists five other characteristics of the Christian view:

(1) It is not carried out by sexual reproduction.

(2) Unlike most natural processes that just happen to living organisms with little or no choice on their part, it is voluntary insofar as we can refuse what God has offered to us.

(3) The new spiritual life (Zoe) is not transmitted by heredity but by the "good infection" from Christ who is the first instance of the New Man.

(4) The speed of this Next Step, rather than a slow gradual change, has been like a flash of lightning and we are still only at the infant stage.

(5) The last characteristic, maturing, has multiple points and is worth looking at in more detail.

1.   Until we rise and follow Christ what are we? (para. 9)

2.   The risen new men are now dotted all over the earth and some are already recognizable. What are they like? (para. 10)

3. How is losing 'ourselves' to become new men like being exposed to light and/or salt? (para. 11,12)

4. Lewis claims there are no real Personalities other than in God and until we give ourselves up to Him we will not have a real self. Will getting a real self just make us all the same? (para. 15)

Answer Guide available at www.MereChristianity.org

Discussion Notes

APPENDICES FOR 'FURTHER UP AND FURTHER IN'

Appendix 1:
"Anti-intellectualism" in Today's Education, Culture and Church and the Consequences on Christianity

No one grows into a Godliness he or she knows nothing about. The word of God must go through our mind if it's going to change our heart and our life.
Donald S. Whitney
Spiritual Disciples for the Christian Life, 1991

The following quotations come from a variety of individuals communicating over the past several decades. While the collection here is not exhaustive, it is, I believe, inclusive enough to demonstrate that we now live in what is possibly the most anti-intellectual era in the history of Western civilization. This does not mean *non*-intellectual as in a lost capacity to think, but anti-intellectual as in the choice to forfeit the exercise and use of that capacity, as in a lost confidence in truth. Consequently, *shallow-thinking* has become the new "norm" in education, culture and even the church.

Education

Has it ever struck you as odd, or unfortunate, that today, when the proportion of literacy throughout Western Europe is higher than it has ever been, people should become susceptible to the influence of advertisement and mass propaganda to an extent hitherto unheard of and unimagined? Do you put this down to the mere mechanical fact that the press and the radio and so on have made propaganda much easier to distribute over a wide area? Or do you sometimes have an uneasy suspicion that the product of modern educational methods is less good than he or she might be at disentangling fact from opinion and the proven from the plausible?...Is not the great defect of our education today...that although we often succeed in teaching our pupils "subjects," we fail lamentably on the whole in teaching them how to think: they learn everything, except the art of learning...For we let our young men and women go out unarmed, in a day when armor was never so necessary. By teaching them all to read, we have left them at the mercy of the printed word. By the invention of the film and the radio, we have made certain that no aversion to reading shall secure them from the incessant battery of words, words, words. They do not know what the words mean; they do not know how to ward them off or blunt their edge or fling them back; they are a prey to words in their emotions instead of being the masters of them in their intellects.

Dorothy Sayers
The Lost Tools of Learning, 1947

We have lived to see the second death of ancient learning. In our time something which was once the possession of all educated men has shrunk to being the technical accomplishment of a few specialists...If one were looking for a man who could not read Virgil though his father could, he might be found more easily in the twentieth century than in the fifth.

C.S. Lewis
De Descriptione Temporum, 1955

There is one thing a professor can be absolutely certain of: almost every student entering the university believes, or says he believes, that truth is relative. If this belief is put to the test, one can count on the students' reaction: they will be uncomprehending...When I first noticed the decline in reading during the late sixties, I began asking my large introductory classes...what books really count for them. Most are silent, puzzled by the question. The notion of books as companions is foreign to them...Though students do not have books, they most emphatically do have music. Nothing is more singular about this generation than its addiction to music...It is their passion; nothing else excites them as it does; they cannot take seriously anything alien to music. When they are in school and with their families, they are longing to plug themselves back into their music...My concern here is not with the moral effect of this music—whether it leads to sex, violence, or drugs. The issue here is its effect on education, and I believe it ruins the imagination of young people and makes it very difficult for them to have a passionate relationship to the art and thought that are the substance of liberal education [i.e. the humanities].

Allan Bloom
The Closing of the American Mind, 1987

The National Commission on Excellence in Education (NCEE) reported that the schooling of the average student is barely adequate and that one out of every seven seventeen-year-olds in the United States is functionally illiterate...The illiteracy rate among minority youth may run as high as 40 percent...In 1850...the rate was only 22 percent, and that was counting the slaves. If the slaves were not counted, the illiteracy rate was less than 11 percent, and for large subgroups like male New Englanders, the rate approached zero. It is clear that the crisis we are in is not a necessary state of affairs. Children are taller now than they were two hundred years ago; there is no reason to believe they have shrunk mentally.

Douglas Wilson
Recovering the Lost Tools of Learning, 1991

Forty years ago our nation's schoolchildren were being disciplined for talking, chewing gum, making noise, and running in the halls. Today, the biggest discipline problems are rape, robbery, assault, vandalism, and drug abuse. Is this then what we might call forty years of progress?

Richard Swenson
Margin, 1992

Liberal education once stood for something grand and good: the study of the arts, humanities and sciences with the aim of improving the mind through the acquisition of knowledge and the pursuit of truth. But some of America's most elite colleges and universities have all but abandoned this goal...

[T]he National Association of Scholars (NAS) this week released its 360-page report "What Does Bowdoin Teach?" Bowdoin College is a small private "liberal arts" school in Brunswick, Maine. Its admissions standards are demanding...The cost of tuition, room, board and fees for the school's roughly 1,800 students is hefty: $56,128 for the 2012-13 academic year, a sum that exceeds the annual income for half of all American households.

The school was founded in 1802 and boasts a distinguished cast of graduates, including Nathaniel Hawthorne, Henry Wadsworth Longfellow and U.S. President Franklin Pierce. But as the report's authors...demonstrate, Bowdoin is not the school it once was.

Bowdoin requires all freshmen to take a first-year seminar, which is supposed to provide the gateway to the "critical thinking" skills the college purports to value. Among the 35 courses from which students must pick...The titles alone tell the story: "Fan Fiction and Cult Classics," "Beyond Pocahontas: Native American Stereotypes," "Racism," "Fictions of Freedom," "Sexual Life of Colonialism," "Prostitutes in Modern Western Culture" and "Queer Gardens...

The study also looks at the college's implicit promotion of sexual promiscuity and the 'hook-up' culture among students, which begins during first-year orientation. A play called "Speak About It," which all incoming students must attend, includes what its authors say are autobiographical sketches from current and former Bowdoin students. The play depicts graphic on-stage sexual encounters between heterosexual and gay couples—complete with simulated orgasms. Paradoxically, the Bowdoin community also seems obsessed with preventing sexual assault...

If Bowdoin were unique in its abandonment of traditional liberal education, this study might be of no more than passing interest. What the authors found at Bowdoin, however, exists to some degree at many if not most elite colleges and universities. This study deserves widespread dissemination and discussion...[and] anyone interested in the future of higher education in America should take note.

Our colleges and universities shape the next generation of leaders and citizens, for better or worse. And the country's most elite schools will influence disproportionately who we become as a nation and a people in the future. What has happened to Bowdoin College should matter to all of us.

Linda Chavez
What Has Happened to Liberal Education?
from the Center for Equal Opportunity, 2013

Culture (Society)

There are more television addicts, more baseball and football addicts, more movie addicts...in this country than there are narcotic addicts.

Shirley Chisholm, former US Congresswoman
Testimony to House Select Committee on Crime, 1969

Edward Gibbon (1737-1794) in his Decline and Fall of the Roman Empire (1776-1788) said that the following five attributes marked Rome at its end: first, a mounting love of show and luxury (that is, affluence); second, a widening gap between the very rich and the very poor...third, an obsession with sex; fourth, freakishness in the arts, masquerading as originality, and enthusiasm pretending to be creativity; fifth, an increased desire to live off the state. It all sounds so familiar. We have come a long road since our first chapter, and we are back in Rome.

Francis Schaeffer
How Should We Then Live, 1976

We live in what may be the most anti-intellectual period in the history of Western civilization....We must have passion—indeed hearts on fire for the things of God. But that passion must resist with intensity the anti-intellectual spirit of the world.

R.C. Sproul
"Burning Hearts Are Not Nourished By Empty Heads"
Christianity Today, 1982

At different times in our history, different cities have been the focal point of a radiating American spirit. In the late eighteenth century, for example, Boston was the center of political radicalism that ignited the shot heard round the world...In the mid-nineteenth century, New York became the symbol of the idea of a melting-pot America...In the early twentieth century, Chicago...came to symbolize the industrial energy and dynamism of America...Today, we must look to the city of Las Vegas, Nevada, as a metaphor of our national character and aspiration...For Las Vegas is a city entirely devoted to the idea of entertainment and as such proclaims the spirit of a culture in which all public discourse increasingly takes the form of entertainment...The result is that we are a people on the verge of amusing ourselves to death.

Neil Postman
Amusing Ourselves to Death, 1986

[For two decades we have moved] toward the creation of a sleazoid info-tainment culture in which the lines between Oprah and Phil...New York Post and Newsday, are too often indistinguishable. In this new culture of journalistic titillation, we teach our readers and viewers that the trivial is significant, that the lurid and the loopy are more important than real news. We do not serve our readers and viewers, we pander them...For the first time in our history the weird and the stupid and the coarse are becoming our cultural norm, even our cultural ideal.

Carl Bernstein
"The Idiot Culture"
in *The New Republic*, 1992

As we approach the twenty-first century, it doesn't take a rocket scientist to recognize that our entire culture is in trouble. We are staring down the barrel of a loaded gun, and we can no longer afford to act like it's loaded with blanks.

Recently, the guidance counselor at a local public high school near my home confessed to a parents' group that the teenagers that have attended the school during the last ten years are the most dysfunctional, illiterate group he has witnessed in close to forty years at the same school. Our society has replaced heroes with celebrities, the quest for a well-informed character with the search for a flat stomach, substance and depth with image and personality. In the political process, the make-up man is more important than the speech writer...The mind-numbing, irrational tripe that fills TV...is digested by millions of bored, lonely Americans hungry for that sort of stuff. What is going on here? What has happened to us?

J. P. Moreland
Love Your God With All Your Mind, 1997

I am not just speaking, as one might think, of the outré fantasies that divert the average supermarket-tabloid reader and New Age spiritualist—the space-alien autopsies, Elvis sightings, two-headed babies, comet-watching suicide cults, photographed guardian angels, government-suppressed cancer cures, global corporate conspiracies, and other gaudy hallucinations at which the 'educated' elite sneer. The hopelessly ignorant we have with us always. Rather, I am concerned...with the more respectably received ideas that many of those same 'educated' folk believe and repeat from their privileged perches in universities, in the media, and especially in popular culture. These are the 'thinking people' whom Thomas Sowell the columnist recently has called the 'anointed,' the caretakers of the 'prevailing vision' that is rarely 'confronted with demands for empirical evidence.' Those ideas are the plagues of the mind, the intellectual diseases creating the new epidemic of false knowledge...

Bruce S. Thornton
Plagues of the Mind, 1999

The Church

There is no longer a Christian mind...the Christian mind has succumbed to the secular drift with a degree of weakness unmatched in Christian History...There is no longer a Christian mind. There is still, of course, a Christian ethic, a Christian practice, and a Christian spirituality...But as a thinking being, the modern Christian has succumbed to secularization.

Harry Blamires
The Christian Mind, 1963

I find myself wondering how the apostle [Paul] would react if he were to visit Western Christendom today. I think he would deplore...the contemporary lack of a Christian mind...I was thankful to hear Dr. Billy Graham say, when addressing some six hundred ministers in London in November, 1970, that if he had his ministry all over again he would study three times as much as he had done. "I've preached to much and studied too little," he said.

> John Stott
> Your Mind Matters, 1972

We are having a revival of feelings but not of the knowledge of God. The church today is more guided by feelings than by convictions...We value enthusiasm more than informed commitment.

> Gallop Poll on Religion, 1980

I must be frank with you: the greatest danger confronting American evangelical Christianity is the danger of anti-intellectualism...For the sake of greater effectiveness in witnessing to Jesus Christ himself, as well as for their own sakes, evangelicals cannot afford to keep on living on the periphery of responsible intellectual existence.

> Ambassador Charles Malik
> "The Other Side of Evangelism"
> *Inaugural Address: Billy Graham Center*, 1980

One thing I noticed about Evangelicals is that they do not read. They do not read the Bible, they do not read the great Christian thinkers, they have never heard of Aquinas. If they're Presbyterian, they've never read the founders of Presbyterianism. As a Jew, that's confusing to me. The commandment to study is so deep in Judaism that we immerse ourselves in study. God gave us a brain, aren't we to use it in his service? When I walk into an Evangelical Christian's home and see a total of 30 books, most of them best-sellers, I do not understand. I have bookcases of Christian books and I am a Jew. Why do I have more Christian books than 98 percent of Christians in America?

> Dennis Prager
> "A Civilization That Believes in Nothing"
> in *The Door*, 1990

Evangelicals have been deeply sinful in being anti-intellectual ever since the 1820s and 1830s. For the longest time we didn't pay the cultural price because we had the numbers, the social zeal, and the spiritual passion for the gospel. But today we are beginning to pay the cultural price. And you can see that most evangelicals simply don't think. For example, there has been no serious evangelical public philosophy in this century...Evangelicals need to repent of the refusal to think christianly and to develop the mind of Christ.

Os Guinness
"Persuasion for the New World: An Interview"
in the *Crucible*, 1992

The scandal of the evangelical mind is that there is not much of an evangelical mind...American evangelicals are not exemplary for their thinking, and they have not been so for several generations.

Mark Noll
The Scandal of the Evangelical Mind, 1994

"I want to ask you my $64,000 question. It's something I've asked each speaker"...There was an audible gasp. A rush of attention swept the room...[that] included many of the big names in American Christendom...But the interest was also because of the questioner. Slim, svelte, and tanned, she was a striking blond in her late twenties who would clearly look just as much at home on a California beach as in the packed seminar room... "How is your body?" she blurted out. Somewhat taken aback at her $64,000 question, I was silent for a few seconds and then—almost without thinking—replied: "Madame, I'm English. How's your mind?"

Os Guinness
Fit Bodies, Fat Minds, 1994

In too many churches, a questing mind can be a plague to its owner. The thinking woman or man seldom gets much support today—and more often than not meets with resistance and suspicion. This is true, not only for those inclined to dig deeply for a more reasoned, better founded faith, but for the Christian who is laboring out in the world to resolve debates and value-clashes in fields like social justice, medical research, education, law, and finance. And so, the Christian who must use his or her mind, because they are driven by the joy of using it, can exist in an odd, ambivalent relationship with his brothers and sisters in Christ. This should not be. Why have we lost, or neglected, the ability to discipline the mind for Christ?

David Hazard
The Christian and the Well Formed Mind
Forward, *Love Your God with All Your Mind*, 1997

Two major developments emerged in the late nineteenth century that contributed to the loss of the Christian mind in America. The [intellectual] legacy of the Pilgrims and Puritans waned, and two new movements emerged from which the evangelical church has never fully recovered...

1. <u>The emergence of anti-intellectualism</u>. During the middle 1800's, three awakenings broke out in the United States: the Second Great Awakening (1800-1820), the revivals of Charles Finney (1824-1837), and the Layman's Prayer Revival (1856-1858). Much good came from these movements. But their overall effect was to overemphasize immediate personal conversion to Christ instead of a studied period of reflection and conviction; emotional, simple, popular preaching instead of intellectually careful and doctrinally precise sermons; and personal feelings and relationship to Christ instead of a deep grasp of the nature of Christian teaching and ideas. Sadly, as historian George Marsden notes, 'Anti-intellectualism was a feature of American revivalism.'

Obviously, there is nothing wrong with the emphasis of these movements on personal conversion. What was a problem, however, was the intellectually shallow, theologically illiterate form of Christianity that came to be...Thousands of people were "converted" to Christ by revivalist preaching, but they had no real intellectual grasp of Christian teaching. As a result, two of the three major American cults began...among the unstable, untaught 'converts': Mormonism (1830) and the Jehovah's Witnesses (1884)...

2. <u>Evangelical withdrawal began</u>. Sadly, the emerging anti-intellectualism in the church created a lack of readiness for the widespread intellectual assault on Christianity that reached full force in the late 1880s. This attack was part of the war of ideas raging at that time and was launched from three different areas. First, certain philosophical ideas from Europe, especially the views of David Hume (1711-1776) and Immanuel Kant (1724-1804), altered people's understanding of religion...Second, German higher criticism of the Bible called its historical reliability into question...Third, Darwinian evolution emerged and 'made the world safe for atheists'...[and] challenged the early chapters of Genesis for some and the very existence of God for others.

Instead of responding to these attacks with a vigorous intellectual counterpunch, many believers grew suspicious of intellectual issues altogether. To be sure, Christians must rely on the Holy Spirit in their intellectual pursuits, but this does not mean they should expend no mental sweat of their own in defending the faith.

...This withdrawal from the broader, intellectual culture and public discourse contributed to the isolation of the church, the marginalization of

Christian ideas from the public arena, and the shallowness and trivialization of Christian living, thought, and activism. In short, culture became saltless.

More specifically, we now live in an evangelical community so deeply committed to a certain way of seeing the Christian faith that this perspective is now within us at a subconscious level. This conceptualization of the Christian life is seldom brought to conscious awareness for debate and discussion....I cannot overemphasize the fact that this modern understanding of Christianity is neither biblical nor consistent with the bulk of church history.

J. P. Moreland
Love Your God with All Your Mind, 1997

The Consequences on Christianity

If we do not use the mind which God has given us, we condemn ourselves to spiritual superficiality.

John Stott
Your Mind Matters, 1972

Many Christians remain in bondage to fears and anxieties simply because they do not avail themselves of the Discipline of study. They may be faithful in church attendance and earnest in fulfilling their religious duties and still they are not changed. I am not here speaking only of those who are going through mere religious forms, but of those who are genuinely seeking to worship and obey Jesus Christ as Lord and Master...the tenor of their lives remains unchanged. Why? Because they have never taken up one of the central ways God uses to change us: study.

Richard Foster
Celebration of Discipline, 1978

Perhaps at no prior moment in history...have so many Christians waged the battle for piety and holiness so lackadaisically and failed so consistently in their quest for righteousness.

George Barna & William McKay
Vital Signs, 1984

We are spiritual dwarfs. A much-traveled leader, a native American (be it said), has declared that he finds North American Protestantism...to be 3000 miles wide and half an inch deep.

J. I. Packer
A Quest for Godliness, 1990

Gallop and Barna hand us survey after survey demonstrating that evangelical Christians are as likely to embrace lifestyles every bit as hedonistic, materialistic, self-centered, and sexually immoral as the world in general.

Michael Horton
"Beyond Culture Wars"
in *Modern Reformation*, 1993

The open secret of many "Bible-believing" churches is that only a very small percentage of their members study the Bible with even the degree of interest, intelligence or joy they bring to bear upon their favorite newspaper or magazine.

Dallas Willard
Hearing God, 1993

This was the cry of one clergyman who whispered to me following a meeting with pastors, "Nobody knows this, but I'm operating on fumes. I am lonely, hollow, shallow, enslaved to a schedule that never lets up." As I embraced him and affirmed his vulnerability and honesty, he began to weep with deep, heaving sobs. We prayed before he slipped back into the crowd. "Lonely, hollow, shallow, and enslaved to a schedule"...those words have haunted me...

Charles Swindoll
Intimacy with the Almighty, 1996

According to the Gallop surveys, 94 percent of Americans believe in God and 74 percent claim to have made a commitment to Jesus Christ. About 34 percent confess to a 'new birth' experience. These figures are shocking when thoughtfully compared to statistics on the same group for ethical behavior, crime, mental distress and disorder, family failures, addictions, financial misdealings, and the like...Are we to suppose that in fact Jesus has no substantial impact on our 'real lives'?

Dallas Willard
The Divine Conspiracy, 1998

My study of discipleship in America has been eye-opening. Almost every church in our country has some type of discipleship program or set of activities, but stunningly few churches have a church of disciples.

George Barna
Growing True Disciples, 2001

"We made a mistake." [Response to a large study which showed that the Willow Creek Community Church model had failed to produce spiritually mature Christians]

Bill Hybels, Pastor and Megachurch founder
Quoted in *World Magazine,* Nov., 2007

One of the great problems in churches today is the perpetual immaturity of the members. Too many Christians grow old without growing up. It is possible to attend church your entire life and never grow into Chirstlike maturity.
Rick Warren
Forward, *The Kingdom Life,* 2010

The above quotations demonstrate that anti-intellectualism has not only permeated today's world but also today's church. Again, this does not mean that human beings have recently experienced a species-wide drop in IQ or world-wide decline in education. What it means is that, in the flurry of today's distracting mass-exposure to everything trivial, inane and superficial, we have stopped thinking about anything significant, far-sighted and of depth; not a mental inactivity, but a mental over-activity in things unimportant. We have ceased to immerse ourselves in the timeless truths, beliefs, and convictions that have previously transformed the lives of individuals in every era since Christ. We have ceased to think as Christ thought: we have ceased to exercise the mind of Christ. The resulting shallowness—in both conviction and conduct—is the epidemic of our times: "Superficiality is the curse of our age...The desperate need today is...for deep people."[12]

Appendix 2:
The Law of Human Nature around the World[13]

The following illustrations of the Natural Law [Law of Human Nature] are collected from such sources as come readily to the hand of one who is not a professional historian. The list makes no pretence of completeness...

C.S. Lewis
The Abolition of Man, 1947

I. The Law of General Beneficence

(a) Negative

'I have not slain men.' (Ancient Egyptian. From the Confession of the Righteous Soul. 'Book of the Dead.' v. *Encyclopedia of Religion and Ethics* [=ERE], vol. v, p. 478.)

'Do not murder.' (Ancient Jewish. Exodus xx.13.)

'Terrify not men or God will terrify thee.' (Ancient Egyptian. Precepts of Ptahhetep. H. R. Hall, *Ancient History of Near East*, p. 133 n.)

'I have not brought misery upon my fellows. I have not made the beginning of every day laborious in the sight of him who worked for me.' (Ancient Egyptian. Confessions of Righteous Soul. ERE v. 478.)

'I have not been grasping.' (Ancient Egyptian. Ibid.)

'Who mediates oppression, his dwelling is overturned.' (Babylonian. Hymn to Samas. ERE v. 455.)

'He who is cruel and calumnious has the character of a cat.' (Hindu. Laws of Manu. Janet, *Histoire de la Science Politique*, vol. i, p. 6.)

'Slander not.' (Babylonian. *Hymn to Samas*. ERE v. 445.)

'Thou shalt not bear false witness against thy neighbor.' (Ancient Jewish. Exodus xx. 16.)

'Utter not a word by which anyone could be wounded.' (Hindu. Janet, p.7.)

'Has he...driven an honest man from his family? Broken up a well cemented clan?' (Babylonian. List of Sins from incantation tablets. ERE v. 466.)

'I have not caused hunger. I have not caused weeping. (Ancient Egyptian. ERE v. 478.)

'Never do to others what you would not like them to do to you.' (Ancient Chinese. *Analects of Confucius*, trans. A. Waley, xv.23; cf. xii. 2.)

'Thou shalt not hate thy brother in thy heart.' (Ancient Jewish. Leviticus xix. 17.)

'He whose heart is in the smallest degree set upon goodness will dislike no one. (Ancient Chinese. *Analects*, iv. 4.)

(b) Positive

'Nature urges that a man should wish human society to exist and should wish to enter it.' (Roman. Cicero, *De Officiis*, I. iv.)

'By the fundamental Law of Nature Man [is] to be preserved as much as possible.' (Locke, *Treatises of Civil Govt*. ii. 3.)

'When the people have multiplied, what next should be done for them? The Master said, Enrich them. Jan Ch'iu said, When one has enriched them, what next should be done for them? The Master said, Instruct them.' (Ancient Chinese, *Analects*, xiii. 9.)

'Speak kindness...show good will.' (Babylonian. *Hymn to Samas.* ERE v. 445.)

'Men were brought into existence for the sake of men that they might do one another good.' (Roman. Cicero, *De Off*. I. vii.)

'Man is man's delight.' (Old Norse. *Havamal* 47.)

'He who is asked for alms should always give.' (Hindu. Janet, i.7.)

'What good man regards any misfortune as no concern of his?' (Roman. Juvenal, xv. 140.)

'I am a man: nothing human is alien to me.' (Roman. Terence, *Heaut. Tim.*)

'Love thy neighbour as thyself.' (Ancient Jewish. Leviticus xix. 18.)

'Love the stranger as thyself.' (Ancient Jewish. *Ibid*. 33, 34.)

'Do to men what you wish men to do to you.' (Christian. Matt. Vii. 12.)

II.   The Law of Special Beneficence

'It is upon the trunk that a gentleman works. When that is firmly set up, the Way grows. And surely proper behaviour to parents and elder brothers is the trunk of goodness.' (Ancient Chinese. *Analects*,i. 2.)

'Brothers shall fights and be each others' bane.' (Old Norse. Account of the Evil Age before the World's end, *Volospa* 45.)

'Has he insulted his elder sister?' (Babylonian. List of Sins. ERE v. 446.)

'You will see them take care of their kindred [and] the children of their friends...never reproaching them in the least.' (Redskin. Le Jeune, quoted ERE v. 437.)

'Love thy wife studiously. Gladden her heart all thy life long.' (Ancient Egyptian. ERE v. 481.)

'Nothing can ever change the claims of kinship for a right thinking man.' (Anglo-Saxon. *Beowulf*, 2600.)

'Did not Socrates love his own children, though he did so as a free man and as one not forgetting that the gods have the first claim on our friendship?' (Greek. Epictetus, iii.24.)

'Natural affection is a thing right and according to Nature.' (Greek, *Ibid*. I. xi.)

'I ought not to be unfeeling like a statue but should fulfill both my natural and artificial relations, as a worshipper, a son, a brother, a father, and a citizen.' (Greek, *Ibid*. III. ii.)

'This first I rede thee: be blameless to thy kindred. Take no vengeance even though they do thee wrong.' (Old Norse. *Sigrdrifumal*, 22.)

'Is it only the sons of Atreus who love their wives? For every good man, who is right-minded, loves and cherishes his own.' (Greek. Homer, *Iliad*. Ix. 340.)

'The union and fellowship of men will be best preserved if each receives from us the more kindness in proportion as he is more closely connected with us.' (Roman. Cicero, *De Off*. I. xvi.)

'Part of us is claimed by our country, part by our parents, part by our friends.' (Roman. *Ibid*. I. vii.)

'If a ruler...compassed the salvation of the whole state, surely you would call him Good? The Master said, It would no longer be a matter of "Good." He would without doubt be a Divine Sage.' (Ancient Chinese. *Analects*, vi. 28.)

'Has it escaped you that, in the eyes of gods and good men, your native land deserves from you more honour, worship and reverence than your mother and father and all your ancestors? That you should give a softer answer to its anger than to a father's anger? That if you cannot persuade it to alter its mind you must obey it in al quietness, whether it binds you or beats you or sends you to a war where you may get wounds or death?' (Greek. Plato, *Crito*, 51 A.B.)

'If any provides not for his own, and especially for those of his own house, he hath denied the faith.' (Christian. I. Tim. v. 8.)

'Put them in mind to obey magistrates.'...'I exhort that prayers be made for kinds and all that are in authority.' (Christian. Tit. iii. 1 and I Tim. ii. 1, 2.)

III. **Duties to Parents, Elders, Ancestors**

'Your father is an image of the Lord of Creation, your mother an image of the Earth. For him who fails to honour them, every work of piety is in vain. This is the first duty.' (Hindu. Janet, i.9.)

'Has he despised Father and Mother?' (Babylonian. List of Sins. ERE v. 446.)

'I was a staff by my Father's side....I went in and out at his command.' (Ancient Egyptian. Confession of the Righteous Soul. ERE v. 481.)

'Honour thy Father and thy Mother.' (Ancient Jewish. Exodus xx.12.)

'To care for parents.' (Greek. List of duties in Epictetus, III. vii.)

'Children, old men, the poor, and the sick, should be considered as the lords of the atmosphere.' (Hindu. Janet, i.8.)

'Rise up before the hoary head and honour the old man.' (ancient Jewish. Lev. xix. 32.)

'I tended the old man, I gave him my staff.' (Ancient Egyptian. ERE v. 481.)

'You will see them take care...of old men.' (Redskin. Le Jeune, quoted ERE v. 437.)

'I have not taken away the oblations of the blessed dead.' Ancient Egyptian. Confession of the Righteous Soul. ERE v. 478.)

'When proper respect toward the dead is shown at the end and continued after they are far away, the more force [te] of a people has reached its highest point.' (Ancient Chinese. *Analects*, i. 9.)

IV. **Duties to Children and Posterity**

'Children. The old, the poor, etc., should be considered as lords of the atmosphere,' (Hindu. Janet, i. 8.)

'To marry and to beget children.' (Greek. List of duties. Epictetus, III. vii.)

'Can you conceive an Epicurean commonwealth?...What will happen? Whence is the population to be kept up? Who will educate them? Who will be Director of Adolescents? Who will be Director of Physical Training? What will be taught?' (Greek. *Ibid.*)

'Nature produces a special love of offspring' and 'To live according to Nature is the supreme good.' (Roman. Cicero, *De Off.* I. iv, and *De Legibus*, I. xxi.)

'The second of these achievements is no less glorious than the first; for while the first did good on one occasion, the second will continue to benefit the state forever.' (Roman. Cicero, *De Off.* I. xxii.)

'Great reverence is owed to a child.' (Roman. Juvenal, xiv. 47.)

'The Master said, Respect the young.' (Ancient Chinese. *Analects*, ix. 22.)

'The killing of the women and more especially of the young boys and girls who are to go to make up the future strength of the people, is the saddest part...and we feel it very sorely.' (Redskin. Account of the Battle of Wounded Knee. ERE v. 432.)

V.   The Law of Justice

(a) Sexual Justice

'Has he approached his neighbour's wife?' (Babylonian. List of Sins. ERE v. 446.)

'Thou shalt not commit adultery.' (Ancient Jewish. Exodus xx. 14.)

'I saw in Nastrond (=Hell)...beguilers of others' wives.' (Old Norse. *Volospa* 38, 39.)

(b) Honesty

'Has he drawn false boundaries?' (Babylonian. List of Sins. ERE v. 446.)

'To wrong, to rob, to cause to be robbed.' (Babylonian. *Ibid.*)

'I have not stolen.' (Ancient Egyptian. Confession of Righteous Soul. ERE v. 478.)

'Thou shalt not steal.' (Ancient Jewish. Exodus xx. 15.)

'Choose loss rather than shameful gains.' (Greek. Chilon Fr. 10. Diels.)

'Justice is the settled and permanent intention of rendering to each man his rights.' (Roman. Justinian, *Institutions*, I. i.)

'If the native made a "find" of any kind (e.g. an honey tree) and marked it, it was thereafter safe for him, as far as his own tribesmen were concerned, not matter how long he left it.' (Australian Aborigines. ERE v. 441.)

'The first point of justice is that none should do any mischief to another unless he has first been attacked by the other's wrongdoing. The second is that a man should treat common property as common property, and private property as his own. There is no such thing as private property by nature, but things have become private either through prior occupation (as when men of old came into empty territory) or by conquest, or law, or agreement, or stipulation, or casting lots.' (Roman. Cicero, *De Off.* I. vii.)

(c) Justice in Court, &c.

'Whoso takes no bribe...well pleasing is this to Samas.' (Babylonian. ERE v. 445.)

'I have not traduced the slave to him who is set over him.' (Ancient Egyptian. Confession of Righteous Soul. ERE v. 478.)

'Thou shalt not bear false witness against thy neighbour.' (Ancient Jewish. Exodus xx. 16.)

'Regard him whom thou knowest like him whom thou knowest not.' (Ancient Egyptian. ERE v. 482.)

'Do no unrighteousness in judgement. You must not consider the fact that one party is poor nor the fact that the other is a great man.' (Ancient Jewish. Leviticus xix. 15.)

VI.   The law of Good Faith and Veracity

'A sacrifice is obliterated by a lie and the merit of alms by an act of fraud.' (Hindu. Janet, i. 6.)

'Whose mouth, full of lying, avails not before thee: thou burnest their utterance.' (Babylonian. Humn to Samas. ERE v. 445.)

'With his mouth was he full of *Yea*, in his heart full of *Nay*.' (Babylonian. ERE v. 446.)

'I sought no trickery, nor swore false oaths.' (Anglo-Saxon. *Beowulf.* 2839.)

'The Master said, Be of unwavering good faith.' (Ancient Chinese, *Analects*, viii. 13.)

'In Nastrond (=Hell) I saw the perjurers.' (Old Norse. *Volospa* 39.)

'Hateful to me as are the gates of Hades is that man who says one thing, and hides another in his heart.' (Greek. Homer, *Iliad*, ix. 312.)

'The foundation of justice is good faith.' (Roman. Cicero, *De Off*. I. vii.)

'[The gentleman] must learn to be faithful to his superiors and to keep promises.' (Ancient Chinese, *Analects*, I. 8.)

'Anything is better than treachery.' (Old Norse. *Havamal* 124.)

VII.   The Law of Mercy

'The poor and the sick should be regarded as lords of the atmosphere.' (Hindu. Janet, i. 8.)

'Whoso makes intercession for the weak, well pleasing is this to Samas.' (Babylonian. ERE v. 445.)

'Has he failed to set a prisoner free?' (Babylonian. List of Sins. ERE v. 446.)

'I have given bread to the naked, a ferry boat to the boatless.' (Ancient Egyptian. ERE v. 478.)

'There, Thor, you got disgrace, when you beat women.' (Old Norse. *Harbarthsljoth* 38.)

'In the Dalebura tribe a woman, a cripple from birth, was carried about by the tribespeople in turn until her death at the age of sixty-six.'...'They never desert the sick.' (Australian Aborigines. ERE v. 443.)

'You will see them take care of...widows, orphans, and old men, never reproaching them.' (Redskin. ERE v. 439.)

'Nature confesses that she has given to the human race the tenderest hearts, by giving us the power to weep. This is the best part of us.' (Roman. Juvenal, xv. 131.)

'They said that he had been the mildest and gentlest of the kings of the world.' (Anglo-Saxon. Praise of the hero in *Beowulf*, 3180.)

'When thou cutest down thine harvest...and hast forgot a sheaf...thou shalt not go again to fetch it: it shall be for the stranger, for the fatherless, and for the widow.' (Ancient Jewish. Deut. xxiv. 19.)

VIII.   The Law of Magnanimity

A.

'There are two kinds of injustice: the first is found in those who do an injury, the second in those who fail to protect another from injury when they can.' (Roman. Cicero, *De Off.* I, vii.)

'Men always knew that when force and injury was offered they might be defenders of themselves; they knew that howsoever men may seek their own commodity, yet if this were done with injury unto others it was not to be suffered, but by all men and by all good means to be withstood.' (English. Hooker, *Laws of Eccl. Polity*, 1. ix. 4.)

'To take no notice of a violent attack is to strengthen the heart of the enemy. Vigour is valiant, but cowardice is vile.' (Ancient Egyptian. The Pharaoh Seunsert III. cit. H. R. Hall, *Ancient History of the near East*, p. 161.)

'They came to the fields of joy, the fresh turf of the Fortunate Woods and the dwellings of the Blessed...here was the company of those who had suffered wounds fighting for the fatherland.' (Roman. Virgil, *Aen.* Vi, 638-9, 660.)

'Courage has got to be harder, heart the stouter, spirit the sterner, as our strength weakens. Here lies our lord, cut to pieces, our best man in the dust. If anyone thinks of leaving this battle, he can howl forever.' (Anglo-Saxon. *Maldon*, 312.)

'Praise and imitate that man to whom, while life is pleasing, death is not grievous.' (Stoic Seneca, *Ep.* Liv.)

'The Master said, Love learning and if attacked be ready to die for the Good Way.' (Ancient Chinese. *Analects*, viii. 13.)

B.

'Death is to be chosen before slavery and base deeds.' (Roman. Cicero, *De Off.* I. xxiii.)

'Death is better for every man than life with shame.' (Anglo-Saxon. *Beowulf*, 2890.)

'Nature and Reason command that nothing uncomely, nothing effeminate, nothing lascivious be done or thought.' (Roman. Cicero, *De Off.* I. iv.)

'We must not listen to those who advise us "being men to think human thoughts, and being mortal to think mortal thoughts," but must put on immortality as much as is possible and strain every nerve to live according to that best part of us, which, being small in bulk, yet much more in its power and honour surpasses all else.' (Ancient Greek. Aristotle, Eth. *Nic.* 1177 B.)

'The soul then ought to conduct the body, and the spirit of our minds the soul. This is therefore the first Law, whereby the highest power of the mind requireth obedience at the hands of all the rest.' (Hooker. *Op. cit.* I. viii. 6.)

'Let him not desire to die, let him not desire to live, let him wait for his time...let him patiently bear hard words, entirely abstaining from bodily pleasures.' (Ancient Indian. Laws of Manu. ERE ii. 98.)

'He who is unmoved, who has restrained his senses...is said to be devoted. As a flame in a windless place that flickers not, so is the devoted.' (Ancient Indian. *Bhagavad gita*. ERE ii. 90.)

C.

'Is not the love of Wisdom a practice of death?' (Ancient Greek. Plato, Phaedo, 81 A.)

'I know that I hung on the gallows for nine nights, wounded with the spear as a sacrifice to Odin, myself offered to Myself.' (Old Norse, Havamal, 1. 10 in Corpus Poeticum Boreale; stanza 139 in *Hildebrand's Lieder der Alteren Edda*. 1922.)

'Verily, verily I say to you unless a grain of wheat falls into the earth and dies, it remains alone, but if it dies it bears much fruit. He who loves his life loses it.' (Christian. John xii. 24, 25)

Appendix 3:
Rival Conceptions of God

Do not believe every spirit, but test the spirits to see whether they are from God;
because many false prophets have gone out into the world.
1 John 4:1

Decision Flow Chart[14]

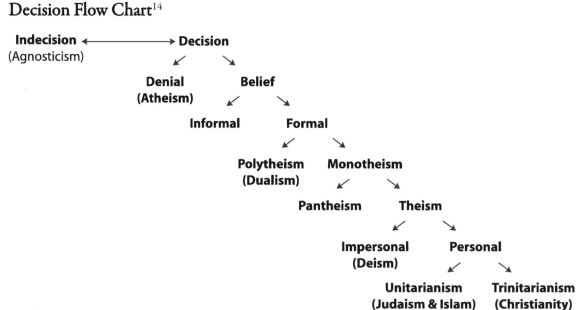

Definitions [15]

Indecision or the inability to decide may be due to genuine obstacles including a lack of information or a misunderstanding; but it may also result from a *decision* not to know or not to search out an answer.

Agnosticism derives its name from two Greek words: "*a*" which means "no" and "*gnosis*" which means "knowledge." An agnostic then is a person who has *no knowledge* about the existence of God. There are two varieties: benign and malignant. A benign agnostic is simply one who confesses he possesses no knowledge about God and who may or may not be open to further inquiry. A *malignant* agnostic is much different. When he says, "I possess no knowledge of God..." he also includes, "...because it is *impossible* for anyone to have knowledge of God."

Decision denotes arriving at a conclusion with a degree of confidence. *Confidence* is perhaps the best single, contemporary term for "faith." *A decision that either denies or believes in the existence of God requires faith.*

Denial of the existence of God is a conclusion which is confident that no facts, reasoning or experience exists that can alter that conclusion. Even if the conclusion does not alter, the confidence may wax and wane (e.g. "There are no atheists in foxholes."). Denial of the "spiritual" or "supernatural" means all questions of origin, reality, purpose, right and wrong, and destiny must be limited to and answered from within the "natural" realm.

Atheism is also a derivative of two Greek words, "*a*" and "*theos*" which means "no god." Whereas agnosticism denies that God is *knowable*, it does not deny that God *exists*. Atheism, on the other hand, denies both claiming that if God does not exist, He cannot be known. There are two consequences of atheism. The first has to do with reality: if there is no God or mind or intelligence behind the universe, then the bottom line is just "matter, time and chance." This is called *materialism* or *naturalism*. The second consequence has to do with morality or ethics. If there is no God, then there is no real right or wrong. With no real right and wrong, one is left with making up his own right and wrong which may constantly change, be in conflict with others, etc. A life that has *existence* but no underlying moral *essence* is meaningless or purposeless. This is called *existentialism*.

Belief in the existence of God is a conclusion which is confident that no facts, reasoning or experience exists that can alter that conclusion. Even if the conclusion does not alter, the confidence may wax and wane (e.g. Heb 10:35 "Therefore, do not throw away your confidence, which has great reward."). Belief in the "spiritual" or "supernatural" means all questions of origin, reality, right and wrong, purpose and destiny may be answered without the limits imposed by "naturalism."

Informal belief means belief that is only instinctive, individualistic or idiosyncratic and not necessarily shared with any other person or group of persons. Graucho Marx comes to mind: "I wouldn't be a member of any club that would have me."

Formal belief is belief that is commonly held and largely agreed upon with other individuals or groups. It is sometimes referred to as "institutionalized" religion by detractors, but "organized" or "established" are probably better adjectives because they denote belief that is acknowledged both broadly in numbers and over time in duration.

Polytheism is derived from "*poly*" or "many" and "*theos*" or "god" and means "many gods." The term was coined to refer to the religious beliefs and practices of ancient Mesopotamia, Egypt, Greece, Rome, and Scandinavia. Polytheistic religions generally considered their deities to be metaphysically finite with each god having only limited authority over specific parts of nature or society such as the underworld, the oceans, fertility, war, etc. Today, Mormonism is the closest thing to a formal polytheism.

Dualism can be classified as polytheistic but essentially has only two deities. The two deities are equal, co-existing powers that oppose one another and fight for control of the universe. While providing an explanation for good and evil, dualism fails as an ethical system because each god thinks it is the good one and an ultimate right and wrong for man cannot be determined. Dualism is found in the ancient Indo-Iranian religion of Zoroastrianism and possibly the Gnostic mystery religions.

Monotheism believes there is one infinite Being or God. Evolutionary theorists in the late 1800s hypothesized that as primitive cultures developed from families and clans to monarchies, their views of God "evolved" from animism (i.e. non-physical spirits that *animated* trees, animals and humans) to polytheism (multiple gods) and finally to monotheism (one supreme God). According to the evolutionary hypothesis, monotheistic societies would at some point begin to realize that religion is a dead-end street and become scientific naturalist. However—as reports came in from anthropologists, sociologists and missionaries around the world, it was discovered that even the most primitive peoples possessed, not animistic or polytheistic beliefs, but monotheistic beliefs of a God who created the world—the naturalistic, evolutionary hypothesis was unsubstantiated by fact.

Pantheism is derived from "*pan*" which means "all" and "*theos*" which means "god"—"all is god" or "everything is god." Rather than God being "outside" of his creation, God is his creation: God and the universe are "one." In that trees are god, fish are god, cows are god and so on, pantheists do not view God as an intellectual being. If "all is one," then particular things, animals and persons ultimately have no individuality but are mere manifestations of God. Examples of pantheists include Hindus, Stoics, Hegel, Spinoza and Einstein. Of note, Buddhism grew out of Hindu origins. Instead of an "all is one" view, Buddhism sees ultimate reality as "all is nothing" or "void of distinction." Particular things, animals, persons, etc. are therefore perceived as *illusions* and not manifestations of God.

Theism or "*theos*" means "god." The prime belief of theism is that God is an un-created, self-existent Being who is outside of time and space and distinct from his creation. He is all-powerful, all-knowing and all-present throughout his creation.

Impersonal does not mean that God is not a person; it means he does not personally interact with his creation.

Deism is simply "watered down" theism. It holds that God exists but that he does not interfere with his creation. He is like a clockmaker who wound up his clock and then left it to run down on its own. Deism provides an origin for the universe and the laws of nature, but then conveniently avoids such things as sin, judgment, hell, repentance and salvation. It is more a religious *philosophy* than a religion and consequently many deists were not particularly moral giants. Deism originated with the Enlightenment (mid-1700s) unlike most other views of God that have noteworthy antecedents in antiquity. Adherents include Benjamin Franklin, Thomas Jefferson and Mark Twain.

Personal means that God is a person and he personally interacts with his creation. He wants a relationship with us and has created us for this purpose. He wants us to pray to him and he wants to communicate back to us.

Unitarianism is a form of theism that posits "God is one Being who exists as one Person." Judaism and Islam are both theistic *unitarian* religions. [Please note that "theistic unitarianism" is not to be confused with the Unitarian Church, the Unity School of Christianity or the Unification Church of the Reverend Sun Moon.]

Trinitarianism is a form of theism that posits "God is one Being, but He exists in three Persons." Whereas one might reason—from the order he finds in nature or the moral "ought" he experiences in his conscience—that God must exist, one would be hard pressed to reason that He must exist in three Persons. Most biblical scholars agree that the trinitarian understanding of God is the direct result of revelation and not of reason or some other source. Thus, the Trinity of Christianity is not objectively provable apart from the Word of God. If the Trinity is a difficult or mysterious concept to grasp, then one probably has it right! While it is difficult to express what the Trinity is, it is not difficult to say what it isn't. The Trinity is <u>not</u> *Tri-theism* or three separate Gods. The Trinity also is <u>not</u> *Tri-modalism* or one God in three manifestations, in which case the expressed love and fellowship within the Trinity would be mere narcissism topped off with a multiple personality disorder! The Trinity as revealed in Scripture is one God in three Persons (the Person of the Father, the Person of Jesus Christ and the Person of the Holy Spirit). God reveals his "personalness" to the utmost by personally entering His creation and *personally* entering the lives of believers yet without ceasing to be God.

Appendix 4:
Made for Each Other: the Gospel and the World

Part I. A Gospel Prepared for the World

The Scripture, foreseeing that God would justify the Gentiles by faith, preached the gospel beforehand to Abraham, saying, "All the nations will be blessed in you." So then those who are of faith are blessed with Abraham, the believer.
Galatians 3:8-9

It is easy to think of the Bible as being two separate and distinct parts: one part pre-gospel (Old Testament) and one part post-gospel (New Testament). But this is a superficial and erroneous understanding. A more truthful analysis is that the *entire* Bible is a record of the ongoing work of God that is called the "gospel." The transition from Old Testament to New Testament is predominantly a transition of intended audience (one people group verses all people groups) rather than a transition of intended message (pre-gospel message verses post-gospel message). The importance of this distinction is as follows.

The gospel was God's plan from "before the foundation of the world" (Ephesians 1:4-6). In other words, it originated before time or space or matter; it existed *before* existence. The gospel was not God's "Plan B" after the failure of some other original plan. The gospel was God's *original* plan. From the very start, it was His original plan for non-automaton, non-robotic, non-puppet human beings in the possession of their own wills to personally move into the world and lives of those He created; a plan to move His very Presence from heaven to a hill, from a hill to a house, from a house to a Human, from that Human to our hearts, and from our hearts to holiness or God-likeness. From the beginning, the gospel was prepared for the world, the whole world, to make man the image-bearer of his Creator (Genesis 1:26).

Dr. Ralph Winters, past director of the U.S. Center for World Missions, stated that the theme of the whole Bible is missions: "Most Christians think that the Bible doesn't really emphasize missions. They see it as an afterthought Christ had at the very end of His ministry...But as a matter of fact the Bible actually begins with missions, maintains missions as its central theme throughout, and climaxes in the Apocalypse with spontaneous outbursts of joy because the missionary mandate has been fulfilled...The main theme of the Bible is God blessing all peoples of the Earth with a blessing first given to Abraham. And where does God promise to bless all peoples of the Earth through Abraham? In Genesis chapter 12. Genesis chapter 12 then is the real beginning of the Bible. Everything prior to Genesis 12 is the introduction. Equally inspired, yes! But the introduction nonetheless."[16]

The Old Testament

The Old Testament appears to only be a Jewish testament, but closer examination reveals otherwise. Many Old Testament narratives involve various sons and daughters of Abraham being blessings to non-Jewish (i.e. Gentile) peoples.[17]

Abraham himself bore witness to *Canaanites*, *Philistines*, *Hittites* and, rather negatively, to *Egyptians*.

Joseph made up for his forefather's poor witness to *Egypt* and blessed the whole *Egyptian nation* in many ways.

Spies from the tribes of Israel who entered Jericho became a blessing to Rahab, a *Canaanite* harlot, and her family.

Naomi was a blessing to two *Moabite* women, Ruth and Orpah.

Moses became a blessing to Jethro, his *Midianite* father-in-law.

King David caused even his enemies, the *Philistines*, to acknowledge God's greatness.

Elijah the prophet was a blessing to a *Sidonian* widow in Zarephath.

Elisha the prophet was a blessing to Naaman, a *Syrian*.

Jonah, however reluctantly, became a blessing to the entire population of *Nineveh*.

King Solomon was a blessing to the *Sabaean* "Queen of the South."

Daniel and his three colleagues, **Shadrach**, **Meshach** and **Abednego**, were a blessing to the *Babylonians*.

Esther and her uncle **Mordecai** were a blessing to the entire *Persian Empire*.

Ezekiel, Jeremiah, Ezra, Nehemiah, Jonah and others declared the Word of God to various *Gentile nations*.

These narratives are selective and, no doubt, recorded for us for God's sovereign purposes; but there have also probably been many thousands of other events throughout history that have not been recorded. Nevertheless, the Old Testament is not a testament for Jewish descendents alone. There are over 300 declarative Old Testament passages that amplify God promise to bless all people.[18] Note here a small sampling:

Psalm 117:1-2 Praise the Lord, all nations [*i.e. Gentiles*]; Laud Him all peoples! For his lovingkindness is great toward us, and the truth of the Lord is everlasting. Praise the Lord!

Isaiah 49:6 He says, "It is too small a thing that You should be My Servant to raise up the tribes of Israel...I will also make You a light to the nations [*i.e. Gentiles*] so that My salvation may reach the ends of the earth."

Psalm 67:1-3 God be gracious to us and bless us, and cause His face to shine upon us—that Your way may be known on the earth, Your salvation among all nations [*i.e. Gentiles*]. Let the peoples praise You, O God; let all the peoples praise You.

The New Testament (Gospels)

In the Gospels, Christ is often delighted by the response of non-Jewish Gentiles He encountered:

Matthew 15:22-28 A Canaanite woman from that region came out and began to cry out saying, "Have mercy on me, Lord, Son of David; my daughter is cruelly demon-possessed." But He did not answer her a word. And His disciples came and implored Him, saying, "Send her away, because she keeps shouting at us." But He answered and said, "I was sent only to the lost sheep of the house of Israel." But she came and began to bow down before Him, saying, "Lord, help me." And He answered and said, "It is not good to take the children's bread and throw it to the dogs." But she said, "Yes, Lord; but even the dogs feed on the crumbs which fall from the their masters' table." Then Jesus said to her, "O woman, your faith is great; it shall be done for you as you wish." And her daughter was healed at once.

Matthew 8:8-10 But the centurion said, "Lord, I am not worthy for You to come under my roof, but just say the word and my servant will be healed. For I also am a man under authority, with soldiers under me; and I say to this one, 'Go!' and he goes, and to another, 'Come!' and he comes, and to my slave, 'Do this!' and he does it." Now when Jesus heard this, He marveled and said to those who were following, "Truly I say to you, I have not found such great faith with anyone in Israel."

The New Testament (Epistles)

In the letter to the Galatians, Paul emphasizes the unbreakable connection between the Abrahamic Covenant and the New Testament gospel no less than five times:

Galatians 3:8 The Scripture, foreseeing that God would justify the Gentiles by faith, preached the gospel beforehand to Abraham, saying, "All the nations will be blessed in you."—Paul saw that the gospel had been preached 2000 years before to Abraham.

Galatians 3:13-14 Christ redeemed us...in order that in Christ Jesus the blessing of Abraham might come to the Gentiles.—Paul connects Christ's redemption with the blessings of Abraham.

Galatians 3:16 Now the promises were spoken to Abraham and his seed. He does not say, "And to seeds," as referring to many but rather to one, "and to your seed," that is Christ.—Paul specifically identifies the seed of Abraham as Christ.

Galatians 3:19 [The Law] was added...until the seed would come to whom the promise had been made.—Paul again identifies the seed and God's promise with Christ.

Galatians 3:29 If you belong to Christ, then you are Abraham's descendents, heirs according to the promise.—Paul identifies all believers in Christ as the actual descendents of Abraham by God's promise.

Part II. A World Prepared for the Gospel

In the past, He let all nations go their own way.
Yet He has not left them without a testimony.

- Acts 14:16-17

When Charles Darwin, in 1859, championed his principles of a progressive evolution to explain how complex biological forms may have originated and emerged from simpler forms, other scholars began applying the same principles to their fields of study with the hope of finding the evolved origins of other phenomena. One such area was the origin of human society, culture and religion.[19]

In 1865 and 1871, Edward Tylor published two volumes called *Primitive Culture: Researches into the Development of Mythology, Philosophy, Religion, Art and Custom* and *Primitive Culture*. The works dominated the field for the next three decades and was completely unassailable to all challengers. In it, Tylor dismissed the Bible's claim that the first religion to appear on earth was monotheistic. Instead, he theorized that primitive savages had first imagined they possessed a "soul" when they wondered about things like sleep, dreams and death. Then they began to think that other entities—animals, trees, rivers, and the sky—were similarly endowed and so spiritism (or "animism"), the first religion, was born. As human society stratified into classes, Tylor next hypothesized that "aristocratic gods" came to be seen as ruling over the run-of-the-mill spirits. Thus, polytheism, the second religion, came about. Finally, in cultures where a supreme monarch came into power—and *only* there—monotheism evolved to become the third and final religion.

From that point, people began to see that religion was a dead-end street and ideas of God, spirits, and souls would be abandoned.[20]

For Tylor's hypothesis to be correct, primitive cultures could not possess any monotheistic presuppositions. It would also tax the hypothesis for a polytheistic religion without a dominant cultural monarchy to have monotheistic inclinations. As it happened, Tylor's "favorite pupil," Andrew Lang, allowed himself to read a missionary's report about primitive inhabitants who already acknowledged the existence of a Supreme Creator God before the missionary had arrived. At first Lang thought there was a mistake, but further investigations brought him more and more examples of similar findings from all around the world. In 1898, he published these findings in a book called The Making of Religion. Nevertheless, the academic community maintained a silent response and Lang was ignored and largely ostracized. In 1912, the year Lang died, Wilhelm Schmidt, an Austrian Catholic priest, took up Lang's cause and published a mammoth volume entitled, The Origin of the Concept of God. As the data kept pouring in, he published another volume, and then another, and then another until, by 1955, he had accumulated more than 4000 pages of evidence in 12 large volumes.[21]

Below is just a small sample of literally hundreds of cases in which our world was prepared beforehand for the Gospel of a loving monotheistic God. I have included a few accounts from the New Testament, but the rest are from the past 150 years or so.

Mediterranean - Greece

● The Greek city of Athens had had a vast number of polytheistic gods for centuries. This greatly distressed Paul when he saw its multitude of idols. He began reasoning with the Jews and God-fearing Greeks (Acts 17:16-17), not likely because they practiced idolatry, but rather because they had not stood against it. Centuries earlier, Xenophanes, Plato and Aristotle—three great *and well-known* Greek philosophers—began using the term *Theos* as the personal name for the one Supreme God. Two centuries later, when the Hebrew Old Testament was translated into Greek, the translators grappled over an appropriate name for God. They decided against the name *Zeus* —the pagan "king of the gods"—and went instead with the philosopher's choice, *Theos*. The name, therefore, should have been familiar to both Hellenistic Jews and Greeks in Athens. Paul adopted *Theos* for his New Testament preaching. When some Athenians remarked that Paul seemed "to be advocating foreign gods" (Acts 17:18), it was the Athenians who were mistaken, not Paul. Furthermore, when Paul was asked to address a meeting of the "Areopagus"—or *Mars Hill Society* of prominent Athenians who met to discuss matters of history, philosophy and religion—he brought up *their own* Athenian alter "to an unknown god" (Acts 17:23). The irony of this was that on the same hill 600 years earlier, a man had been brought to Athens to stop a devastating plague. He succeeded not by appeasing any of the many gods known to the Athenians, but by appeasing the one God unknown to them. The man's name was Epimenides of

Knossos (Crete). He and descriptions of an alter to an unknown god are mentioned in several historical writings (Diogenes Laertius' *The Lives of Eminent Philosophers*; Plutarch's *Life of Solon*; Plato's *Laws*; Aristotle's *The Art of Rhetoric*; Pausanias' *Description of Ancient Greece*; Philostratus' *Appolonius of Tyana*). It was probably as unlikely for an Athenian to not know about Epimenides as it was for a Jew to not know about Moses. Even a *non-Athenian* Jewish convert to Christ like Paul had knowledge of God's use of Epimenides to prepare Athens for the Gospel. Paul called him a prophet and quoted from one of his poems, *Cretica*, twice in the New Testament (Acts 17:28 and Titus 1:12). A monotheistic God had been in the city-state history of polytheistic Athens for six centuries.[22]

● Later, the apostle John continued to use Paul's approach to the Greek philosophical mind. He found a Greek term that dated back to the Greek Stoic philosopher Heraclitus (around 600 B.C.). The term denoted the *divine reason or plan which coordinated the changing universe* and was similar in meaning to the Aramaic term *memra* used by the Jews for the "word" of the Lord. The term Heraclitus used was *Logos* which John equated with Christ in his writings.[23]

Africa

● The Gedeo people of south central Ethiopia shared a common belief in a benevolent, omnipotent Creator of all by the name of *Magano*. However, most of the people were far more concerned about appeasing an evil being they called *Sheit'an*. Why? They sacrificed to *Sheit'an* not because they loved him, but because they simply did not enjoy close enough ties to *Magano* to be done with *Sheit'an*. Around 1940, a Gedeo man named, Warrasa Wange, began pursuing a personal response from *Magano* by praying that He would reveal Himself to the Gedeo. During one of his prayers, he had a vision. He saw two white-skinned strangers come to live in an odd shiny-roofed house under a large sycamore tree at the edge of his villages. Then the odd house began to multiply until several of the houses dotted the entire landscape. He also heard a voice say, "These men will bring you a message from *Magano*, the God you seek. Wait for them." Warrasa waited for eight years during which time other soothsayers among his people prophesied that the strangers would come. Sure enough, in 1948, two Canadian missionaries arrived and lived under the sycamore tree. Today there are over 200 churches among the Gedeo people in their region of Ethiopia.[24]

● *Koro* means "the Creator" in several Bantu languages of Africa. In the Central Africa's Republic, one Bantu tribe—the Mbaka—may have come closer then all others to correctly anticipating not only the arrival of *Koro's* message, but also its content. Missionary Eugene Rosenau, Ph.D., whose father and Baptist colleagues first preached to the Mbaka in the 1920s still marvels at the Mbaka, "Your Mbaka ancestors were closer to the truth than my Germanic forefathers in northern Europe!" The Mbaka related the following story: "Koro, the Creator, sent word to our forefathers long ages ago that He has already sent His Son into the world to accomplish something wonderful for all mankind. Later, however, our forefathers turned away from the truth about Koro's Son. In time they even forgot what it was that He accomplished for mankind. Since the time of 'the forgetting,' successive generations of our people have longed to discover the truth about Koro's Son. But all we could learn was that messengers would eventually come to restore that forgotten knowledge to us. Somehow we knew also that the messengers would probably be white-skinned..."[25]

India

● The Santal are a group of people in India, living in a region north of Calcutta. They were first discovered in 1867 by two missionaries, one of whom was able to quickly learn the Santal language. Being so far removed from Jewish or Christian influences, the missionaries thought it would take years for the Santal to show any interest in the gospel. To their utter amazement, the Santal were electrified at once by the gospel message. One of their sages responded, "This means that Thakur Jiu—or Genuine God—has not forgotten us after all this time." Clearly the missionaries were not introducing a new concept by talking about one Supreme God. When asked why they worshipped demons and spirits, the Santal told of Thakur Jiu creating the first man and woman, their being placed in a garden west of India, a temptation leading nakedness and shame, an eventual flood and the survival of a "holy pair," descendents multiplying, migrating and being divided into many different peoples and then the passage of the Santal predecessors being blocked in the high mountains. They then bound themselves by oaths to appease the "spirits of the great mountains," made it through Khyber Pass, and traveled to where they now had lived for centuries. But their hope remained of someday returning to Thakur Jiu while fearing He had forgotten them.[26]

● The Naga are composed of 24 tribes who live in India, near Burma's northwestern border. They were found to have a clear concept of a "Deity of highly personal character associated with the sky more than the earth" who "stood above all others." They called Him Chepo-Thuru—the God who sustains everything. Among their many traditions are: memorial stones at special places, "first fruit" offerings, blood offerings, holy animal offerings, eating unleavened bread, keeping a sacred fire burning continuously, special regard for the number seven, harvest feasts and the blowing of the trumpet after the harvest. They never depict Chepo-Thuru with an idol.[27]

● The Mizo, another people group living along the India-Burma border (300 miles southwest of the Naga), worship Pathian, the one Supreme God. "Pa" means "father" and "Thian" has the possible interpretation of "holy". Therefore Pathian means "holy father." The Mizo believe Pathian is the "one Supreme God, a God of all humanity and goodness."[28]

Asia

● The Karen of Burma—had a prophecy from "time immemorial" that a "white brother" would bring a "lost book" to them, a book written by the god, Y'wa, the Supreme God, that would set them free from all their oppressors.[29]

● The Kachin (north of Burma)—acknowledge a Creator, *Karat Kasang*, whose "shape or form exceeds man's ability to comprehend." He is sometimes called *Hpan Wa Ningsang*—the Glorious One Who Creates, or *Che Wan Ningchang*—the One Who Knows. The Kachin believe that *Karat Kasang* once gave their forefathers a book which they lost, but which one day would be restored.[30]

● The Kui tribesmen, living along the Thai-Burma border, build houses of worship to the true God in anticipation of the time when a messenger from God would enter the places of worship with the lost book in His hand to teach the people. No idols were allowed or placed in the places of worship.[31]

● The Buddhist peoples of Southeast Asia anticipate the coming of the fifth manifestation of Buddha, called *Phra-Ariya-Metrai*—the Lord of Mercy. His coming is a verbal tradition widespread in Laos, northern Thailand and eastern Burma. The *Metrai* Buddha, unlike all proceeding manifestations of the Buddha that sat cross-legged, is described sitting on a chair or throne.[32]

● The Lahu—between Thailand, China and Laos—have a tradition that *Gui'Sha*—Creator of all things—had given their forefathers his law written on rice cakes. A famine came, and the forefathers ate the sacred rice cakes, rationalizing that the law would be inside them. They could not, however, obey their Creator perfectly until they regained the precise written form of His laws. The Lahu have prophets of *Gui'Sha* whose mission is to keep expectation of help from *Gui'Sha* constantly alive in the peoples' hearts, by reciting proverbs, such as "when the right time comes, *Gui'Sha* himself will send to us a white brother with a white book containing the white laws of *Gui'Sha*—the words lost by our forefathers so long ago."[33]

● The Chinese call him *Shang Ti*—the Lord of Heaven. Some scholars believe this may be related linguistically to the Hebrew term *Shaddai*, as in *El Shaddai*, the Almighty.[34]

● The Lisu of China wait patiently for a white brother with a book of the true God written in the Lisu language, which, oddly, does not have a written alphabet. When they receive this book, they believe that they will have a king of their own to reign over them (they have been ruled by the Chinese for many generations).[35]

● In Korean, he is known as *Hananim*—The Great One. Both *Shang Ti* and *Hananim* predate Confucianism, Taoism & Buddhism by an unknown number of centuries. The *Encyclopedia of Religion and Ethics* states that the first reference to any kind of religious belief in China was to

Shang Ti alone, approximately 2,600 years before Christ, 2,000 years before Confucianism or any other structured religion in China.[36]

Pacific Islands

● The Hawaiians have approximately 20 "cities of refuge" scattered throughout the Hawaiian island chain. These were places of refuge for "defeated warriors, noncombatants, or taboo breakers" who reached the boundaries ahead of their pursuers. Ancient Hebrews, having crossed into the Promised Land, were directed by God through Moses to designate six Hebrew cities—three on each side of the Jordan River—as "cities of refuge" to provide shelter for individuals fleeing from any threat of death by violence (Joshua 20, 21).[37]

● The Yali are black-skinned cannibals of central New Guinea. They live some 5000 miles away from the brown-skinned Hawaiian Polynesians. But they also have *Osuwa* or places of refuge that are off limits to their enemies.[38]

The Americas

● The Incas were ruled from 1438-1471 by King Pachacuti. In the Andes of Peru, he built Machu Picchu, a temple to the sun god *Inti* that would have rivaled Solomon's temple. He wrote psalms of incredible profundity and soaring lyricism. In these, however, he questioned the credentials of the sun god *Inti* conveying that he knew he was worshipping a created thing and not the Creator. King Pachacuti then referred to *Viracocha*, the Lord and omnipotent Creator of all things. *Viracocha* was thought to be a God of great antiquity, and *Viracocha*-like references are prominent throughout North, Central and South American Indian cultures ranging from Alaska to Tierra del Fuego whereas sun worship appears in very few cultures.[39]

● Living deep within the Amazon jungle of Ecuador and all but completely isolated from civilization was a fierce warrior tribe called the Waodani. The tribe was so fierce that it had splintered into warring factions that frequently attacked each other. The life expectancy of the Waodani was obviously not long. Their concept of God did not call for outside strangers bringing them some book or message from God, it merely called for bravery or fearlessness or what the Waodani called, "jumping the boa." Only those who had jumped the boa could see or know God. The first five missionaries to make contact with Waodani were immediately speared to death, but soon afterwards, the surviving families of these were allowed to move in and live among the Waodani. What God had done to begin a change in the fierce hearts of the Waodani took a number of decades for the son of one five dead to understand. In short, the missionaries' bravery was demonstrated to the Waodani by their *ability to see God as they were dying*. For more details, read Steve Saint's *End of the Spear.*[40]

Appendix 5:
Evolution and Thinking (Or Is C.S. Lewis an Evolutionist?)

C.S. Lewis seems to give affirmative nods to evolution in a few places in *Mere Christianity* (e.g., Chapter 5 of Book 2, Chapter 11 of Book 4). Is he an evolutionist?

Although its first radio broadcasts took place in 1941, *Mere Christianity* was not compiled into a final single volume until 1952. By this time in history, the world was abuzz with new scientific discoveries. The universe had suddenly become much older which gave the Theory of Evolution "more time" to take place and therefore more plausibility.

Furthermore, the first "by chance alone" amino acid had been produced—via a very *intelligently designed* laboratory apparatus—and the molecular structure of DNA had been unraveled. These findings gave the Theory of Evolution a new *modus operandi* and moved it from the always murky arguments of Haeckel's fraudulent ontological drawings and the continual paleontological debates about fossil relationships into the bright new realm of molecular biology.

It is within this intellectual academic milieu that C.S. Lewis became and then openly functioned as a Christian.

Whenever he broached topics like nature and evolution, Lewis wisely acknowledged that he was *not* a scientist. He was a specialist in literature, languages and philosophy with a personal fondness for mythology. This meant he was well-read and keenly attuned to the influence of stories, words, reason, thought, morality and myths. He stayed out of the emerging scientific tussles of discovery and dispute and politely tipped his hat. But within his own areas of proficiency, he did not isolate himself from the parley:

> If the solar system was brought about by an accidental collision, then the appearance of organic life on this planet was also an accident, and the whole evolution of Man was an accident too. If so, then all our present thoughts are mere accidents—the accidental by-product of the movement of atoms. And this holds for the thoughts of the materialists and astronomers as well as for anyone else's. But if their thoughts—i.e., Materialism and Astronomy—are merely accidental by-products, why should believe them to be true? I see no reason for believing that one accident should be able to give me a correct account of all other accidents.

C.S. Lewis
Answers to Questions on Christianity, 1944

I come to bury the great Myth of the nineteenth and early twentieth century...

I call it a Myth because it is, as I have said, the imaginative and not the logical result of what is called 'modern science'...

The central idea of the Myth is what its believers would call 'Evolution' or 'Development' or 'Emergence'...I do not mean that the doctrine of Evolution as held by practicing biologists is a Myth. It may be shown, by later biologists, to be a less satisfactory hypothesis than was hoped for fifty years ago. But that does not amount to being a Myth. It is a genuine scientific hypothesis. But we must sharply distinguish between Evolution as a biological theorem and popular Evolutionism or Developmentalism which is certainly a Myth. Before proceeding to describe it and pronounce its eulogy, I had better make clear its mythical character.

We have, first of all, the evidence of chronology. If popular Evolutionism were not a Myth but the intellectually legitimate result of the scientific theorem on the public mind, it would arise *after* that theorem had become widely known. We should have the theorem known first of all to a few, then adopted by all scientists, then spreading to all men of general education, then beginning to effect poetry and the arts, and finally percolating to the mass of people. In fact, however, we find something quite different. The clearest and finest poetic expressions of the Myth come before the *Origin of Species* was published (1859)...Almost before the scientists spoke, certainly before they spoke clearly, imagination was ripe for it.

The finest expression of the Myth in English does not come from Bridges, nor from Shaw, nor from Wells, nor from Olaf Stapledon. It is...Oceanus, in Keats's *Hyperion*, nearly forty years before the *Origin of Species*. And on the continent we have the *Nibelung's Ring* [of Wagner]...The tragedy of the Evolutionary Myth has never been more nobly expressed than in his Wotan: its heady raptures never more irresistibly than in *Siegfried*...

That, then, is the first proof that popular Evolution is a Myth. In making it Imagination runs ahead of scientific evidence. 'The prophetic soul of the big world' was already pregnant with the Myth: if science had not met the imaginative need, science would not have been so popular...

In the second place we have internal evidence...According to [Professor D.M.S. Watson] Evolution "is accepted by zoologists not because it has been observed to occur or...can be proved by logically coherent evidence to be true, but because the only alternative, special creation, is clearly incredible." This would mean that the sole ground for believing it is not empirical but metaphysical...

In the science, Evolution is a theory about *changes*: in the Myth it is a fact about *improvements*. Thus a real scientist like Professor J.B.S. Haldane...adds: "We are therefore inclined to regard progress as the rule of evolution. Actually it is the exception, and for every case of it there ten of degeneration." But the Myth simply expurgates the ten cases of degeneration. In the popular mind the word 'Evolution' conjures up a picture of things moving 'onward and upwards', and of nothing else whatsoever. And it might have been predicted that it would do so. Already, before science had spoken, the mythical imagination knew the kind of 'Evolution' it wanted. It wanted the Keatsian and Wagnerian kind...

[The Myth] gives us almost everything the imagination craves—irony, heroism, vastness, unity in multiplicity and a tragic close. It appeals to every part of me except my reason. That is why those of us who feel that the Myth is already dead for us must not make the mistake of trying to 'debunk' it in the wrong way...For my own part, though I believe it no longer, I shall always enjoy it as I enjoy other myths. I shall keep my Cave-Man where I keep Balder and Helen and the Argonauts: and there often re-visit him.

C.S. Lewis
Funeral of a Great Myth, 1945

The Naturalist cannot condemn other people's thoughts because they have irrational causes and continue to believe his own which have equally irrational causes.

The shortest and simplest form of this argument is that given by Professor J.B.S. Haldane in Possible Worlds. He writes, "If my mental processes are determined wholly by the motions of atoms in my brain, I have no reason to suppose that my beliefs are true...and hence I have no reason for supposing my brain to be composed of atoms"...

All arguments about the validity of thought make a tacit, and illegitimate, exception in favour of the bit of thought you are doing at that moment. It has to be left outside the discussion and simply believed in, in the simple old-fashioned way. Thus the Freudian proves that all thoughts are merely due to complexes except the thoughts which constitute this proof itself. The Marxist proves that all thoughts result from class conditioning—except the thought he is thinking while he say this. It is therefore always impossible to begin with any other data whatever and from them to find out whether thought is valid. You must do the exact opposite—must begin by admitting the self-evidence of logical thought...The validity of thought is central: all other things have to be fitted in round it as best they can.

C.S. Lewis
Miracles: A Preliminary Study, 1947

Granted that Reason is prior to matter...I can understand how men should come, by observation and inference, to know a lot about the universe they live in. If, on the other hand, I swallow the [modern] scientific cosmology as a whole, then not only can I not fit in Christianity, but I cannot even fit in science.

C.S. Lewis
They Asked For a Paper, 1962

No, C.S. Lewis is not an evolutionist and his swordsmanship against it is evident in several of his writings. Nevertheless, he was a great lover of *mythology*.

Appendix 6:
The Purpose of Giving

No one can serve two masters; for either he will hate the one and love the other or he will be devoted to one and despise the other. You cannot serve God and wealth.
Matthew 6:24

In the passage where the New Testament says that every one must work, it gives as a reason "in order that he may have something to give to those in need."
C.S. Lewis
Mere Christianity, 1952

The importance of work is fairly clear to most anyone: we work because we need a way to feed, clothe and put a shelter over ourselves. However, the importance of *giving*, it would seem, is far less apparent—or more people would voluntarily do it.

Three reasons come to my mind when considering the purpose of giving. While each reason has merit, only one is suitable as a virtue or moral practice in the Christian life.

The first reason for giving may be succinctly stated as this: **we freely give to avoid being forced to give**. As societies increase and grow, so do the laws and governing authorities that are necessary to manage and maintain them. An inherent risk, inseparable from the benefit received from such stabilizing governances, is the potential for *too much* government. In extreme cases of this situation, where a tyrant or elitist ruling group comes to power, as personal income vanishes, so does the issues of giving. But in less extreme cases where a free society practices capitalism, socialistic practices may be introduced in order to help those struggling with poverty or other overwhelming needs. Well-organized charitable giving in many cases not only reduces but exceeds the need for "state- sponsored" assistance.

When Lewis states the New Testament hints at a society that is "Leftist" with "no passengers or parasites" and "no manufacture of silly luxuries" and no "sillier advertisements to persuade us to buy them," we must not misinterpret what he means. As he pointed out, the Christian view of *man and society* understands that, though a civilization or nation may last a hundred or even a thousand years, man is *everlasting* and therefore infinitely more valuable. Lewis then is not advocating the Karl Marx "Leftist" ideal of the "state" being greater than the "individual" where all income essentially belongs to the state. He is merely pointing out that even our free-market system that promotes individuality has its own flaws—greed and lack of concern for others—and should not be *ipso facto* regarded as *the* economic system of Christianity.

When Lewis was giving his BBC radio talks, a lot of discussion was taking place as to which political-economic system was best for Britain. Lewis would have been in agreement with the following statements of Winston Churchill (Churchill actually invited Lewis to join his Cabinet). In a 1945 speech, Churchill, concisely clarified the issue at hand: "The inherent vice of capitalism is the unequal sharing of blessings. The inherent virtue of socialism is the equal sharing of miseries."[41] The flaws of capitalism aside, in 1947, Churchill noted that: "You may try to destroy wealth [i.e. redistribute capitalistic assets], and find that all you have done is to increase poverty."[42]

Many years later, after decades of British socialist policies, another Prime Minister, Margaret Thatcher, finally summed it up this way: "Socialist governments...always run out of other people's money."[43] Giving to God in order to avoid giving to Caesar (i.e., taxes) is not an evil motivation but it also is not soundly biblically.

A second possible reason to give is this: **we give in order to receive from God**. This putting-the-cart-before-the-horse perspective needs little explanation but is mentioned here because it has been a widely held and practiced motif in Christendom today. "You can't out give God" is a cry most all of us have heard from pulpits if we have spent any time in contemporary American churches. As a young Christian, I was once unwisely taken in by a "Faith-Promise" program at the church I attended. I was single, had a well-paying night job and had recently purchased my first little fixer-upper house. Tithing 25% percent of my income by "faith-promise to watch God bless" seemed reasonable until I was awaken one day when I heard a non-Christian family member stocking my bare cabinets with food, moving buckets to catch rain water flowing through the leaking roof and then asking me, "So, is this how God blesses you?"

I am not casting stones here but I do believe it is important to note that "prosperity-promises" are largely unheard of in either the churches of developing, non-affluent countries or in the pages of the New Testament:

> Jesus walked away from his conversation with the rich young ruler, saying, "How hard it is for the rich to enter the kingdom of God!" The very next verse says, "The disciples were amazed at his words"...In the dawn of this new phase in redemptive history, no teachers (including Jesus) in the New Testament ever promise material wealth a reward for obedience. As if this were not startling enough to first-century Jews (and twenty-first-century American Christians), we also see no verse in the New Testament where God's people are ever again commanded to build a majestic place of worship. Instead God's people are told to be the temple—the place of worship. And their possessions are to be spent on building, not a place where people can come to see God's glory, but a people who are taking God's glory to the world...Are you and I looking to Jesus for advice that

seems fiscally responsible according to the standards of the world around us? Or are we looking to Jesus for total leadership in our lives, even if that means going against everything our affluent culture and maybe even our affluent religious neighbors might tell us to do?

David Platt
Radical, 2010

Having shown us [in Matthew 5] true well-being and the goodness of the kingdom heart, Jesus now, in Matthew 6, alerts us to the two main things that will block or hinder a life constantly interactive with God and healthy growth in the kingdom. These are to have the approval of others, especially for being devout, and the desire to secure ourselves by means of material wealth. If we allow them to, these two desires will pull us out of the sway of the kingdom—"the range of God's effective will"...—and back into the barren 'righteousness' of the scribe and the Pharisee. But as we keep these two things in their proper place, through a constant, disciplines, and clear-eyed reliance on God, we will grow rapidly in kingdom substance.

Dallas Willard
The Divine Conspiracy, 1998

So what third option do we have with *our* personal wealth while we are still living in a democratic economic system that remains more capitalistic than socialistic?

First, we must understand what the Bible says about "wealth" or having more than enough:

Do not store up for yourselves treasures on earth, where moth and rust destroy, and where thieves break in and steal.

Matthew 6:19

But those who want to get rich fall into temptation and a snare and many foolish and harmful desires which plunge them into ruin and destruction.

1 Timothy 6:9

Second, we must understand whose approval the Bible says we are seeking:

Now the Pharisees, who were lovers of money, were listening to all these things and were scoffing at Him. And He said to them, "You are those who justify yourselves in the sight of men, but God knows the heart; for that which is highly esteemed among men is detestable in the sight of God."

Luke 16:14-15

How can you believe, when you receive glory from one another and you do not seek the glory that is from the one and only God?

John 5:44

If I were still trying to please men, I would not be a bond-servant of Christ.
Galatians 1:10

Our standard for giving should rest with seeking to please and obey the Lord as He reveals Himself to us—it should not be our neighbor or even our *religious* neighbor. Should we choose to use even our religious neighbor as a standard, the picture today is not becoming. In the area of tithing, evangelical denominations have traditionally given more than mainline denominations. Nevertheless, Ronsvalle's annual *The State of Christian Giving* has shown a decline in evangelical tithing from 6.15% of income in 1968 to only 4.0% in 2006. If all American Christians tithed 10%, it is estimated that the annual revenues would be over $140 billion—enough to provide food, general healthcare and education for the entire world with $60-70 billion still remaining for evangelism. However, evangelicals have practiced keeping up with the Jones's more than keeping up with Jesus: "As we got richer and richer, evangelicals chose to spend more and more on themselves and give a smaller and smaller percentage to the church. Today, on average, evangelicals give about two-fifths [40%] of a tithe."[44]

While some of us may be called to sell everything, give it away and trustingly follow Christ, others may be called to earn noteworthy sums of money to support those taking the gospel into the world. I believe Lewis gives a simple little rule to help all of us in this area: "I am afraid the only safe rule is to give more than you can spare. In other words, if our expenditure on comforts, luxuries, amusements, etc., is up to the standard common among those with the same income as our own, we are probably giving away too little. If our charities do not pinch or hamper us, I should say they are too small. There ought to be things we should like to do and cannot do because our charities expenditure excludes them."[45]

I once asked my son, "If God entrusted you with a million dollars, would you take it?" "Of course!" he immediately answered. I then asked, "If God entrusted you with a million dollars to live on but also, at His direction, be a conduit to give to others, would you take it?" That understandably took a little more thought to answer.

Appendix 7:
Producing a "Christian Society"

Caesar hoped to reform men by changing institutions and laws: Christ wished to remake institutions, and lessen laws, by changing men.
Will Durant
The Story of Civilization; III: 562

Christendom may be defined briefly as that part of the world in which, if any man stands up in public and solemnly swears that he is a Christian, all his auditors will laugh.
H.L. Mencken
Prejudices, Fourth Series, 1924

A Christian society is not going to arrive until most of us really want it: and we are not going to want it until we become more fully Christian.
C.S. Lewis
Mere Christianity, 1952

He has made us to be a kingdom...
Revelation 1:6

While Christianity has flourished in times and places where Christian monarchs have reigned or Christian-principled democracies governed, Lewis points out that the New Testament "has not, and does not profess to have, a detailed political programme for...a particular society at a particular moment. It could not have. It is meant for all men at all times and the particular programme which sited one place or time would not suit another."[46] So, how then are we to produce a "Christian society"?

Christendom or Christ?

Over thirty years ago, a British journalist was invited to deliver the inaugural Pascal Lectures on the subject of *Christianity and the University*. The journalist's name was Malcolm Muggeridge. He was the past editor of Britain's well-known *Punch* magazine and had an enduring reputation for being a lifelong, tart-tongued agnostic with the uncanny ability of seeing through the fluff of many of the contemporary issues of his day. Late in his life, he also racked up one other accolade that went against the grain: he ended up a Johnny-come-lately-convert-to-Christ.[47]

In his lectures, Muggeridge drew upon the past writings of a number of historic Christians and contrasted them to what he found within much of present-day Christianity. He then warned that contemporary Christendom—the influence Christianity exerted on society, education and ecclesiastical matters—despite its past successes, was coming to an end![48] He contended that modern Christianity was wrongheaded and not traveling the right path. Muggeridge's warnings did not initially receive significant attention; but slowly over time other voices began to join his:

> It could certainly be argued that any impact that Christianity is having on American culture is largely by God's grace—in spite of his people, not because of them.
>
> George Barna & William McKay
> *Vital Signs*, 1984

> Our age currently finds itself in a crisis of faith. Too many people have only a speculative and not an experiential knowledge of the truth of faith. The reality of God has become hypothetical even for many who call themselves Christians.
>
> Donald Bloesch
> *The Crisis of Piety*, 1988

> The modern age is an age of revolution—revolution motivated by insight into the appalling vastness of human suffering and need...there is an epidemic of depression, suicide, personal emptiness, and escapism through drugs and alcohol, cultic obsession, consumerism, and sex and violence—all combined with an inability to sustain deep and enduring relationships...how does Christianity fit into the answer? Very poorly, it seems, for Christians are among those caught up in the sorrowful epidemic just referred to. And the fact is so prominent that modern thinking has come to view the Christian faith as powerless, even archaic, at the very least irrelevant.
>
> Dallas Willard
> *The Spirit of the Disciplines*, 1988

> Far from living in a world elsewhere, the faithful in the United States are remarkably like everyone else...American culture has triumphed [over faith].
>
> Alan Wolfe
> *The Transformation of American Religion,* 2003

> The cultural captivity of Christianity in the West is nearly complete, and with the religion tamed, it is open season on the West's Christian heritage. I worry about a West without a moral center facing a politically resurgent Islam.

Lamin Sanneh
Interviewed in *Christianity Today*, 2003

The Age of Progress saw Christians of all sorts wage a valiant struggle against the advance of secularism...In spite of Christians' best efforts, however, Christianity was slowly driven from public life in the Western World. Believers were left with the problem we recognize in our own time: How can Christians exert moral influence in pluralistic and totalitarian societies where Christian assumptions about reality no longer prevail?

Bruce S.elley
Introduction and Overview of the History of the Church
The Portable Seminary, 2006

If the 50-year trend continues, projected membership of SBC [Southern Baptist Convention] churches would be 8.7 million in 2050, down from 16.2 million last year [2008]...membership could fall from a peak of 6 percent of the American population in the late 1980s to 2 percent in 2050.

Ed Stetzer, Director, Lifeway Research
in Rob Phillips, "Southern Baptists face further decline"
www.lifeway.com, Oct. 6, 2009

Muggeridge's warnings from thirty years ago were, it must be admitted, if not completely correct then at least not far off in their forecasts. Christendom does indeed appear to be losing its salt and light. But in pointing out the accuracy of his predictions, it must also be noted that Muggeridge's long-ago lectures did not end in pessimism and despair. His *The End of Christendom* lecture was followed by a second lecture titled, *But Not of Christ*.[49] So, Muggeridge's observations had two parts: "The end of Christendom" part *and* the "But not of Christ" part.

Now as alarming and disheartening as *The End of Christendom* part may be—particularly in terms of its waning influence on today's culture, education and even the church—there are many reasons to not focus on it here. Most specifically, for Muggeridge, it really is *not* the important part. The important part is the *But Not of Christ* part. If that is the case, if Christ is the important part, if He is the never-ending-always-enduring part, then, despite of the status of Christendom, the fuller focus of a Christian's attention should be on Christ and, therefore, *on what was most important to Him.*

What Was Most Important To Christ?

What do you think was most important to Christ? Really think about this. Was it His birth? Was it His ministry? Was it His crucifixion or perhaps His resurrection? The answer is, while each of these was important, none of them was the *most* important. I would like to ask a number of other questions to reveal what burned supreme in Christ's heart [Scripture emphases mine]:

1. *From the start*, what did the angel tell Mary about Jesus?

> The angel said to her, "Do not be afraid, Mary; for you have found favor with God. And Behold, you will conceive in your womb and bear a son, and you shall name him Jesus...and His *kingdom* will have no end."
>
> Luke 1:30-31, 33

2. What did Christ's *forerunner*, John the Baptist, preach about?

> John the Baptist came preaching in the wilderness of Judea, saying, "Repent, for *the kingdom of heaven* is at hand."
>
> Matthew 3:1-2

3. What did Christ say His *purpose* was when He began His public ministry?

> But He said to them, "I must preach *the kingdom of God* to other cities also, for I was sent for this purpose."
>
> Luke 4:43

4. What nearly were Christ's *first public words* in each Gospel?

> From that time Jesus began to preach, "Repent, for *the kingdom of heaven* is at hand."
>
> Matthew 4:17

> And after John had been taken into custody, Jesus came into Galilee, preaching the gospel of God, and saying, "The time is fulfilled, and *the kingdom of God* is at hand; repent and believe in the gospel."
>
> Mark 1:14-15

> But He said to them, "I must preach *the kingdom of God* to other cities also, for I was sent for this purpose."
>
> Luke 4:43

> Jesus answered and said to him, "Truly, truly, I say to you, unless one is born again, he cannot see *the kingdom of God*."

John 3:3

5. What *gospel* did Christ proclaim?

> And Jesus was going about in all Galilee teaching in their synagogues, and proclaiming *the gospel of the kingdom*...
>
> Matthew 4:23

> And Jesus was going about all the cities and villages, teaching in their synagogues, and proclaiming *the gospel of the kingdom*...
>
> Matthew 9:35

> And Jesus answered and said to them, "And this *gospel of the kingdom* shall be preached in the whole world for a witness to all the nations, and then the end shall come."
>
> Matthew 24:4, 14

> ...Jesus came into Galilee, preaching the gospel of God, and saying, "The time is fulfilled, and *the kingdom of God* is at hand; repent and believe in the gospel."
>
> Mark 1:14-15

> The Law and the Prophets were proclaimed until John; since then *the gospel of the kingdom* is preached, and everyone is forcing his way into it.
>
> Luke 16:16

6. What did Christ preach His *longest recorded sermon* about?

> Matthew 5:1-7:29 records Christ's longest sermon, the "Sermon on the Mount." Its main theme is *the kingdom of heaven*, which is repeated 9 times in the sermon.

7. In the only *prayer model* He gave, before our daily bread, forgiveness of sin and deliverance from temptation, what did Christ say we should pray for?

> *Thy kingdom* come, Thy will be done.
>
> Matthew 6:10

8. What did Christ state that our *number one priority* should be?

> "But seek first *His kingdom* and His righteousness"
>
> Matthew 6:33

9. What one subject is the most frequent focus of Christ's *parables*?

Of the 51 identified parables of Christ, 18 specifically address and another 7 are in reference to *the kingdom of God*; thus, it the subject of at least 25 out of 51 parables, more than any other subject.

10. When Christ sent out the *twelve*, what did He instruct them to preach?

These twelve Jesus sent out after instructing them, saying, "Do not go in the way of the Gentiles, and do not enter any city of the Samaritans; but rather go to the lost sheep of Israel. And as you go, preach, saying, '*The kingdom of heaven* is at hand.'"

Matthew 10:5-7

11. When Christ sent out the *seventy*, what did He instruct them to preach?

Now after this the Lord appointed seventy others, and sent them two and two ahead of him to every city and place where He himself was going to come. And He was saying...."And whatever city you enter and they receive you, eat what is set before you; and heal those in it who are sick, and say to them, '*The kingdom of God* has come near you."

Luke 10:1-2, 8-9

12. At the beginning of Acts—between His resurrection and ascension—what did Christ speak about when *He appeared to His disciples over a period of forty days*?

To these He also presented Himself alive, after His suffering, by many convincing proofs, appearing to them over a period of forty days, and speaking of the things concerning *the kingdom of God*.

Acts 1:3

13. Throughout Acts—after Christ's ascension—what did His *followers* proclaim and teach?

But when they believed Philip preaching the good news about *the kingdom of God* and the name of Christ, they were being baptized, man and woman alike.

Acts 8:12

And [Paul] entered the synagogue and continued speaking out boldly for three months, reasoning and persuading them about *the kingdom of God*.

Acts 19:8

And now, behold, I [Paul] know that all of you [Ephesians], among whom I went about preaching *the kingdom*, will see my face no more...Therefore be on the alert, remember that night and day for a period of three years I did not cease to admonish each one with tears.

Acts 20:25, 31

14. At the end of Acts, what did *Paul continue to preach* under house arrest to all who came to Him?

> And [Paul] stayed two full years in his own rented quarters, and was welcoming all who came to him, preaching *the kingdom of God*, and teaching concerning the Lord Jesus with all openness, unhindered.
>
> Acts 28:30-31

What Has Happened To The Kingdom of God?

Does it come as a surprise that the answer to each of these questions is the same and that *before, during and even after* His public ministry the single-most important concern and focus of Christ —"the kingdom of God"—never changes? Then, even more surprising, note the following statements:

> How does it come to pass that, with open Bibles before them, men and women should be wrong not so much about certain details with respect to the Gospel, but about the whole thing, about the very essence of the Gospel?...it is indeed very surprising that at the end of the twentieth century, men and women should still be all wrong about what the Gospel is; wrong about its foundation, wrong about its central message...the gospel of Jesus Christ is the same as the gospel of the kingdom of God. It is in the coming of this Person that the kingdom of God has come.
>
> D. Martyn Lloyd-Jones
> *The Kingdom of God*, from sermons preached in 1963

> How much have you heard here about the Kingdom of God? Not much. It is not in our language. But it was Jesus' prime concern.
>
> Michael Green
> Lausanne Conference on World Evangelism, 1974

> During the past sixteen years I can recollect only two occasions on which I have heard sermons specifically devoted to the theme of the Kingdom of God....I find this silence rather surprising because it is universally agreed by New Testament scholars that the central theme of the teaching of Jesus was the Kingdom of God.
>
> Dr. I. Howard Marshall,
> Bible expositor, University of Aberdeen
> *The Expository Times*, October, 1977

When was the last time you heard a sermon on the Kingdom of God? Frankly, I'd be hard put to recall ever having heard a solid exposition of this theme. How do we square this silence with the widely accepted fact that the Kingdom of God dominated our Lord's thought and ministry? My experience is not uncommon. I've checked this out with my colleagues. Of course, they readily agree they've often heard sermons on bits and pieces of Jesus' parables. But as for a solid sermon on the nature of the Kingdom of God as Jesus taught it—upon reflection, they too began to express surprise that [it] is the rare pastor who tackles the subject.

Arthur Glasser, expert on Christian missions
Missiology, April, 1980

I cannot help wondering out loud why I haven't heard more about it in the thirty years I have been a Christian. I certainly read about it enough in the Bible....But I honestly cannot remember any pastor whose ministry I have been under actually preaching a sermon on the Kingdom of God. As I rummage through my own sermon barrel, I now realize that I myself have never preached a sermon on it. Where has the Kingdom been?

Peter Wagner, Movement Leader
Worldwide "Church Growth" movement
Church Growth and the Whole Gospel, 1981

We who profess Christianity will believe what is constantly presented to us as gospel. If gospels of sin management are preached, they are what Christians will believe. And those in the wider world who reject those gospels will believe that what they have rejected is the gospel of Jesus Christ himself—when, in fact, they haven't yet heard it....The souls of human beings are left to shrivel and die on the plains of life because they are not introduced into the environment for which they were made, the living kingdom of eternal life.

Dallas Willard, Chair and Professor
School of Philosophy, USC
The Divine Conspiracy, 1998

Contemporary evangelism and indeed preaching in general, though supposedly based on the Bible, *do not sound like the teaching of Jesus*. While they continue to use His name, they do not reflect his central theme—the Kingdom of God...To make sense of what Jesus taught, we must understand the term "Kingdom of God" as he understood it.

Sir Anthony Buzzard, theologian
The Coming of Kingdom of the Messiah, 2002

While the Kingdom of God was the central theme of all preaching in the New Testament, it has been virtually ignored by modern-day evangelists. The absence of Kingdom-centered evangelism has had devastating effects on the Western church and has now reached critical mass....The deficiency is so great that most evangelists and professors of evangelism would be hard-pressed even to define the 'gospel of the kingdom' (Matthew 24:14; Mark 1:14). The result has been a watered-down message that has no power to change lives.

> R. Alan Streett, Chair and Professor of
> Evangelism
> *Evangelism & the Kingdom of God*
> Baptist Press, April 2, 2004

Based on what he saw in contemporary Christianity, when Muggeridge proclaimed as eminent "The End of Christendom" yet also "But Not of Christ," did he actually mean Christ and His inseparable connection to the Gospel of the Kingdom of God? I believe so, because a few years before he had written this: "Jesus's good news, then, was that the Kingdom of God had come, and that he, Jesus, was its herald and expounder to men. More than that, in some special, mysterious way, he *was* the Kingdom."[50]

If the kingdom of God is inseparable from Christ and the foremost of His priorities, it is not a stretch to conclude that it is also foundational to all Christ did and all He commanded His disciples to do—even for producing a "Christian Society." Therefore, it is essential that we have a firm understanding of the kingdom of God [Scripture emphases mine]:

Where is the Kingdom of God?

> The Lord has established His throne in the *heavens*, and His sovereignty rules over all.
>
> Psalm 103:19

> Thus says the Lord, "*Heaven* is My throne."
>
> Isaiah 66:1

> [T]hat you [King Nebuchadnezzar] be driven away from mankind...until you recognize that the Most High is ruler over the realm of mankind...after you recognize that it is *Heaven* that rules.
>
> Daniel 4:25-26

> The Lord is in His holy temple; the Lord's throne is in *heaven*.
>
> Psalm 11:4 (*a psalm of David*)

> He who is enthroned in the *heavens* laughs, the Lord scoffs at them.

Psalm 2:4

Repent, for the kingdom of heaven is *at hand.*

Matthew 3:2

Whatever city you enter and they receive you, eat what is set before you; and heal those in it who are sick, and say to them, "The kingdom of God has come *near to you.*"

Luke 10:8-9

But if I cast out demons by the finger of God, then the kingdom of God has come *upon you.*

Luke 11:20

The kingdom of God is not with signs to be observed; nor will they say, "Look, here it is!" or "There it is!" For behold, the kingdom of God is *in your midst.*

Luke 17:20-21

Quote:

Where is the kingdom of God? Comprehensive theological studies have debated the complexities of this question for centuries, but let me suggest a simplified answer from Scripture: The kingdom of God is wherever Jesus is king! If Jesus is king *in your heart,* then the kingdom of God is in within you (see Luke 17:21). Because Jesus is king *in heaven,* then the kingdom of God is also in heaven (see Psalm 103:19). While Jesus walked the earth, He used miracles to announce that the kingdom of God was with them (see Luke 11:20), and when the reign of Christ is fully realized on earth, then the kingdom of God is on earth (see Revelation 5:10).

Rick Warren
Forward to *The Kingdom Life,* 2010

What is the Kingdom of God?

My kingdom is *not of this realm.*

John 18:36

For the kingdom of God is not eating and drinking, but righteousness and peace and joy *in the Holy Spirit.*

Romans 14:17

"Your kingdom come, *Your will be done...*"

Matthew 6:10

Quotes:

They are mistaken who think the Kingdom of God means Heaven. It is rather the spiritual life, which is begun by faith in this world and daily increases according to the continual progress of faith.

John Calvin
The Gospel According to St. John, 1555

If you have not chosen the Kingdom of God first, it will in the end make no difference what you have chosen instead...Nothing has separated us from God but our own will, or rather our own will is our separation from God.

William Law
A Serious Call to a Devout and Holy Life, 1728

The kingdom of heaven is not even come when God's will is our law; it is fully come when God's will is our will.

George MacDonald
Unspoken Sermons, 1867-89

The one and only law of life that sets a man free from all the forces that blight and destroy is the Will of God. Show me a man who lives for one day wholly, utterly, in word and thought and deed in the Will of God, and I will show you a man who is antedating heaven, and who for that day reaches the plane of life which at once broadest, freest, and gladdest...[Christ's] Sermon on the Mount is the Magna Charta of the Will of God, the most wonderful words that ever fell on the ears of man.

G. Campbell Morgan
God's Perfect Will, 1901

There is often a desire to understand more fully just how we may know the will of God. To this it may be answered: *First*, His leading is only for those who are already committed to do as He may choose. To such it may be said, "God is able to speak loud enough to make a *willing* soul hear." *Second*, The divine leading will always be according to the Scriptures...*Third*, He does not lead His children by any rules whatsoever. No two of His children will be led alike and it is most probable that He will never lead any one of His children twice in exactly the same way. Therefore rules are apt to be misleading. True spirituality consists in a life which is free from law and which is lived, to the minutest detail of individuality, by the power of the Spirit. *Fourth*, The divine leading is by the Spirit who indwells the Christian...True spirituality is a reality. It is *all* of the manifestations of the Spirit in and through the one in whom He dwells. He manifests in the believer the life of Christ. He came not to reveal Himself but to make Christ real *to* the heart, and *through* the heart, of man.

Lewis Sperry Chafer
He That Is Spiritual, 1918

But I didn't come to understand the kingdom through theologians. I came to the understanding when I was a young Baptist Minister. I noticed that I spent a lot of my time trying to get people to come and hear me, and other ministers did the same. But when I looked at Jesus his problem was getting away from people! So I said there has to be something different here. So I found what every scholar will tell you, that Jesus' message was the kingdom of God. He proclaimed it, he manifested it and he taught it. When he sent out his disciples, he didn't send them out to teach (that's the hard part), but to proclaim and manifest (the easy part). It was very powerful...When you look at the Bible you see that the kingdom of God is God acting. It is the range of God's effective will. When I pray 'thy kingdom come, thy will be done' I am praying first that God's will may be done in my own life and then around me...So as someone who is living in the kingdom, I am praying that this may become a true expression of who I am by inner transformation. Discipleship is learning how to do that.

Dallas Willard
"Kingdom Living"
Christianity+Renewal Magazine, 2002

What is the kingdom of God? It is the rule and reign of God! When we pray, "Thy kingdom come, Thy will be done," we are praying a redundant statement. Whenever God's will is done, the kingdom has come. The two phrases are the same thing. The reason we pray, Thy kingdom come, Thy will be done on earth as it is in heaven" (Matthew 6:10, KJV) is because God's will is done *perfectly* in heaven but imperfectly on earth.

Rick Warren
Forward to *The Kingdom Life*, 2010

How do I enter the kingdom of God?

Truly, truly, I say to you, unless one is *born again* he cannot see the kingdom of God...unless one is *born of water and the Spirit* he cannot enter the kingdom of God.

John 3:3, 5

Not everyone who says to Me, 'Lord, Lord,' will enter the kingdom of heaven, but he who does the *will* of My Father who is in heaven.

Matthew 7:21

But by His doing you are *in Christ Jesus*...

1 Corinthians 1:30

...[T]hey believed Philip preaching the good news [gospel] about the kingdom of God and the *name of Jesus Christ*...

Acts 8:12

Quote:

What's that? The gospel is [also] about the name of Jesus?...What is the name of Jesus? It is access to the kingdom of God. Jesus taught His disciples how to act in His name...In John 1:2 we read, "As many as received Him to them He gave the right [or the authority, if you wish] to become the children of God." John continues, "...even to those who believe in His name who were born, not of blood nor of the will of the flesh [natural abilities] nor the will of man, but of God."

Dallas Willard
The Kingdom Life, 2010

How do I live in it?

Discipline yourself for the purpose of godliness [Christ-likeness].

I Timothy 4:7

Work out your salvation with fear and trembling, for it is God who is at work in you, both to will and to work for His good pleasure.

Philippians 2:12-13

Quote:

There is only one thing you can consecrate to God, and that is your right to yourself (Romans 12:1). If you give God your right to yourself [by seeking His will], He will make a holy experiment out of you. God's experiments always succeed. The one mark of a saint is the moral originality that springs from abandonment to Jesus Christ. In the life of a saint there is this amazing wellspring of original life all the time; the spirit of God is a well of water springing up, perennially fresh. The saint realizes that it is God who engineers circumstances, consequently there is no whine, but a reckless abandon to Jesus. Never make a principle out of your experience. Let God be as original with other people as He is with you.

Oswald Chambers
My Utmost for His Highest

We must never neglect to influence and win the culture and society in which we live, but we must never do this in any way other than God's—no matter how many attractive bells and whistles we come up with. It must be God's way and not our own, God's will and not our own. By increasingly seeking God's will—day by day, hour by hour, moment by moment—He will increasingly transform us into His image-bearers, into greater Christlikeness, into the *gospel incarnate*. In learning to do His will, we will be living in God's *present* kingdom: the influence and effect on those around us will be greater that any political or social program we might otherwise devise by human efforts alone.

Appendix 8:
Psychological Make Up & Choice

"The philosophy of Freud...is in direct contradiction to Christianity: and also in direct contradiction to the other great psychologist, Jung...But psychoanalysis itself, apart from all the philosophical additions that Freud and others have made to it, is not in the least contradictory to Christianity.

C.S. Lewis
Mere Christianity, 1952

There are two extreme opinions within Christianity regarding psychological counseling. One view thinks there is no place at all for psychological therapy in Christianity; the other view thinks that every Christian needs intense psychotherapy (and these are friends within the church not enemies outside!) As a Christian and a physician, I think the right answer rest somewhere in between these two extremes and I agree with Dr. Larry Crabb that the need today is not so much for counseling as it is for spiritual community or *a safe place to hit bottom.* "We all need a place safe enough to embrace our brokenness, our failure, and our inability to cope, and in the midst of torment, a place to again discover life. I spend so much energy refusing to hit bottom...I wonder how many of us never come to grips with how small and helpless we are. Brokenness is not attractive, not until we are broken in a safe place. Until we experience the life of Christ poured into us, perhaps directly by our Father through His Spirit, often through His Word or a song, not frequently enough by our brothers and sisters, until then we don't understand joy."[51]

Many in the world and in the church today are confused, frightened and suffering. We all have 'psychological histories' or 'baggage' we carry around with us. The question is not *whether* we have issues and problems, but *what* we are to do with them. How do we grow into Christ-likeness when our Adam-likeness just will not seem to let us go? I believe the following *chart* from Dr. Craig Ellison is extremely helpful.[52]

Chart Explanation[53]

Before the Fall, man possessed "Ontological Givens" (traits that were part of his *being*) or psycho-spiritual qualities that reflected the image and creative work of God. These included *acceptance, belonging, competence, equity, identity, security, significance and transcendence.* They can be found or inferred from verses in Genesis 1-3 and account for the psychological, social and spiritual characteristics of a fully functioning human being. Taken together, these "givens" made up the healthy, unified, rational True Self God intended for humans.

A Psychospiritual Model of Christian Counseling

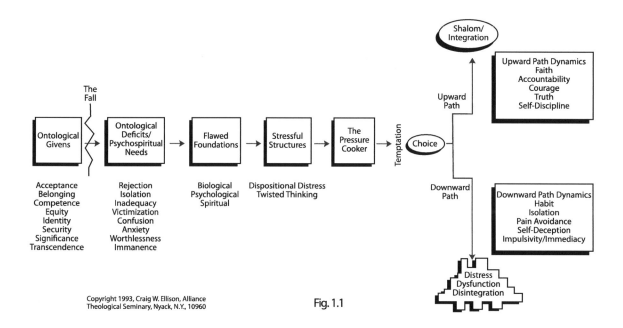

Fig. 1.1

After the Fall, man's nature or *being* was changed. The Ontological Givens became "Ontological Deficits" or "Psycho-spiritual Needs." The True Self that God had intended for humans became an irrational False or Deceived and Deceiving Self that was characterized by painful *rejection or shame, isolation, inadequacy, victimization, confusion, anxiety, worthlessness, and immanence or meaningless and chaos.*

Characteristic patterns of coping with life's stressor as adults are learned in childhood. These may be healthy patterns learned from good spiritual training and nurturing parents, but in settings of increased marital breakdown and family dysfunction, the patterns can be unhealthy. Other factors during childhood and adolescence such as physical and/or sexual abuse, illnesses, and alcohol and drug exposure, etc. may, on top of post-Fall deficits, add "Flawed Foundations" to an individual. These may be *biological, psychological or spiritual* flaws that affect how we cope with the stresses of adult life.

Every human being is unique with his or her own *disposition* or personality. How these develop in life can greatly vary, ranging from a balanced hardiness in meetings life's challenges to unbalanced extremes of victimization and dependency on one hand and Type A personalities and perfectionism on the other. Furthermore, *twisted thinking* in our belief systems can lead to "faulty filters" and "rotten rules." Faulty filters are emotionally-anchored beliefs about one's self, relationships, God, and life in general that are false. Rotten rules are *shoulds* and *should nots* that govern a person's choices in unhealthy and unholy ways. When one's disposition and thinking are at odds with our well-being, they are referred to as "Stressful Structures" in Dr. Ellison's chart.

"The Pressure Cooker" is life. The residual stress an individual carries within from his or her "Ontological Deficits," "Flawed Foundations" and "Stressful Structures" steps out and is put to the test. Satan and the world are at their finest here and throw their *temptations* at us. What are we armed with? Choice!

No doubt this all seems overwhelming. But this is exactly where God wants us and where He is working with and helping us. Our choices are making us into new beings: either peaceful, well-integrated beings or distressed dysfunctional beings. Lewis sums it up nicely for us: "People often think of Christian morality as a kind of bargain in which God says, 'If you keep a lot of rules I'll reward you, and if you don't I'll do the other thing.' I do not think that is the best way of looking at it. I would much rather say that every time you make a choice you are turning the central part of you, the part of you that chooses, into something a little different from what it was before. And taking your life as a whole, with all your innumerable choices, all your life long you are slowly turning this central thing either into a heavenly creature or into a hellish one: either into a creature that is in harmony with God, and with other creatures, and with itself, or else into one that is in a state of war and hatred with God, and with its fellow-creatures, and with itself. To be the one kind of creature is heaven: that is, it is joy and peace and knowledge and power. To be the other means madness, horror, idiocy, rage, impotence, and eternal loneliness. Each of us at each moment is progressing to the one state or the other."[54]

Appendix 9:
Hope: Longing for Heaven

As the deer longs for the water brooks, so my soul longs for You, O God.
Psalm 42:1

"A wish may lead to false beliefs, granted. But what does the existence of the wish suggest? At one time I was much impressed by Arnold's line 'Nor does the being hungry prove that we have bread.' But surely, tho' it doesn't prove that one particular man will get food, it does prove that there is such a thing as food! i.e. if we were a species that didn't normally eat, weren't designed to eat, wd. we feel hungry?"

C.S. Lewis
in letter to Sheldon Vanauken, 1950

Lewis defines the virtue of *hope* as a continual looking forward to the eternal world. He then suggested two reasons why many of us find it difficult to want or long for heaven:

The first is that we have not been trained for such. Our modern education has sought to keep our minds focused on (or distracted by?) *this* world.

The second is that when the *real desire for heaven* is present, we often fail to recognize it. Back in the early days of my spiritual searching I went through a great deal of distress trying to sort out what my experiences of "Joy" were. I spoke with a Catholic priest, a Jewish Rabbi, a Zen Roshi, a Hindu meditation leader, a Tibetan Lama, etc. The Catholic priest was the most helpful, but by far the most unfortunate discussion I had was with a polite but very misinformed UCLA football player: he told me he was a "born-again" Christian and had been involved in his family's church most of his life but had never once heard of any Christian having such experiences. He concluded that what I was experiencing, therefore, "Must be satanic."

I therefore have included a few quotes here from Lewis to help illuminate what is meant by "wanting" or "longing for" heaven:

> The experience is one of intense longing...This hunger is better than any other fullness; this poverty better than any other wealth. And thus it comes about, that if the desire is long absent, it may itself be desired, and that new desiring becomes a new instance of the original desire.

C.S. Lewis
Pilgrim's Regress, 1933

In all developed religion we find...what Professor Otto calls the *Numinous*...What is certain is that now, at any rate, the numinous experience exists and that if we start from ourselves we can trace it a long way back.

A modern example may be found (if we are not too proud to seek it there) in the *Wind and Willows* where Rat and Mole approach Pan on the island...

Going back about a century we find copious examples in Wordsworth

...Going back further we get a very hard, pure and strong example in Malory...At the beginning of our era it finds expression in the Apocalypse...In Pagan literature we find Ovid's picture of the dark grove on the Aventine...and Virgil gives us the palace of Latinus...A Greek fragment attributed, but improbably, to Æschylus, tells of earth, sea, and mountain shaking...And further back Ezekiel tells us of the rings in his Theophany...and Jacob raising from sleep says, "How dreadful is this place!"

We do not know how far back in human history this feeling goes...But our main concern is not with its dates. The important thing is that somehow or other it has come into existence, and is widespread, and does not disappear from the mind with the growth of knowledge or civilization.

C.S. Lewis
The Problem of Pain, 1940

The New Testament has lots to say about self-denial, but not about self-denial as an end in itself. We are told to deny ourselves and to take up our crosses in order that we may follow Christ; and nearly every description of what we shall ultimately find if we do so contains as appeal to desire. If there lurks in most modern minds the notion that to desire our own good and earnestly to hope for the enjoyment of it is a bad thing, I submit that this notion has crept in from Kant and the Stoics and is no part of the Christian faith. Indeed, if we consider the unblushing promises of reward and the staggering nature of the rewards promised in the Gospels, it would seem that Our Lord finds our desires, not too strong, but too weak. We are half-hearted creatures, fooling around with drink and sex and ambition when infinite joy is offered us, like an ignorant child who wants to go on making mud pies in a slum because he cannot imagine what is meant by the offer of a holiday at sea. We are far too easily pleased...

In speaking of this desire for our own far-off country...I feel a certain shyness. I am almost committing an indecency. I am trying to rip open the inconsolable secret in each one of you—the secret which hurts so much that you take your revenge on it by calling it names like Nostalgia and Romanticism and Adolescence; the secret also which pierces with such sweetness that when, in very intimate conversation, the mention of it becomes imminent, we grow awkward and affect to laugh; the secret we cannot hide and cannot tell, though we desire to do both.

C.S. Lewis
The Weight of Glory, 1941

In a sense the story of my life is about nothing else....it is that of an unsatisfied desire which is itself more desirable than any other satisfaction. I call it Joy, which is here a technical term and must be distinguished both from Happiness and Pleasure. Joy (in my sense) has indeed one characteristic, and one only, in common with them; the fact that anyone who has ever experienced it will want it again. Apart from that and considered only in its quality, it might almost equally be called a particular kind of unhappiness or grief. But then it is a kind we want. I doubt whether anyone who has tasted it would ever, if both were in his power, exchange it for all the pleasure in the world. But then Joy is never in our power and pleasure often is.

C.S. Lewis
Surprised by Joy, 1955

This final quote is from Andrew Greeley who also references the pioneering academic work done on these experiences by Laski and also Maslow:

It is late at night. A man has driven many miles to a house on the shore of a lake. He parks his car, walks down the steps to a pier jutting out into the water. On this moonless night the man looks up toward the great black umbrella of stars over his head and a feeling of unspeakable peace comes over him. In the next instant of awareness it is morning; he has no idea what happened to all the hours in between.

A young woman has just made love with her husband. They have snatched an interlude together in the middle of the afternoon. It was the best sex they ever had, and she lies exhausted in his arms. Suddenly, a new and very different kind of pleasure takes possession of her. She smiles first and then laughs; her entire body takes on a peculiarly delightful glow. This new pleasure makes intercourse seem mild in comparison. The whole of the universe has somehow flooded her being.

A troubled young man has been listening to Beethoven's Ninth Symphony on a phonograph in his apartment. He turns off the music and begins to work on a term paper, but he makes little progress. The doubts, the fears, the thoughts of self-destruction that have harassed him before return. Then, in counterpoint, he hears the Ode to Joy, and something, perhaps someone, takes possession of the room and of him. The doubts, the fears, the anxieties are dispelled forever; the young man *knows* there is nothing to worry about.

A mother bends over her baby's crib. The child is peacefully asleep, and she notices as though for the first time the shape of his tiny ear. It is the greatest work of art she has ever seen. Peace and joy surge through her, and a pale, misty blue light seems to absorb both her and her child for a time that seems both an instant and eternity.

Something dramatic has occurred in each of these four cases to alter the consciousness of the people involved; and it is something that has happened in all times and in all places of the human condition as we know it. The four people have experienced an interlude of mystical ecstasy...

Whether such experiences are noticed or not is probably a function of whether they are at any given moment culturally acceptable. Abraham Maslow has suggested that almost everyone he studied had some sort of "peak-experience," by which he meant an intense feeling of unity with the universe and of one's own place within that unity. Marghanita Laski, in her pioneering study (based on a nonrepresentative sample), found that 'sensations of transcendent ecstasy' were widespread.

> Andrew M. Greeley
> *Ecstasy A Way of Knowing, 1974*

Appendix 10:
Transformation: From Compatible to Intimate

"Be transformed by the renewing of your mind, that you may prove what the will of God is, that which is good and acceptable and perfect."
Romans 12:2

"We never find out the strength of the evil impulse inside us until we try to fight it...The main thing we learn from a serious attempt to practice the Christian virtues is that we fail. If there is any idea that God had set us a sort of exam and we might get good marks by deserving them, that has to be wiped out...Then comes another discovery. Every faculty you have, your power of thinking or of moving your limbs from moment to moment, is given to you by God...When a man has made these two discoveries God can really get to work. It is after this that real life begins. The man is awake now."
C.S. Lewis
Mere Christianity, 1952

"A key biblical principle for change is this: We don't break habits, we replace them...You are to Put Off your old sinful way of life, renew your mind with the truths of Scripture, and Put On the new godly way of life."
Armand Tiffe
Transformed Into His Likeness, 2005

So we have been "saved"—now what?

Or let me ask that a different way: apart from the Law—apart from the "ought"—by grace through faith, the very righteousness of God has been conferred upon us signifying the credit, honor and respect of a *standard of perfection*, yet why is there still such a lack of inner freedom?

Put it one more way: "I know I have been made *compatible* with You, Lord, but how do I now become *intimate* as well. How do I change?"

The change we are talking about isn't the change from incompatible to God to compatible (i.e. "salvation," "justification," "reconciliation," or "imputed righteousness"); it is the change from compatible to intimate with God (i.e. "sanctification," "growing in grace," "spiritual formation," "becoming godly" or "becoming Christlike"). In biblical terms, this is called "Transformation."

The foundation of transformation—and this *must* be understood for any real progress to be made—has two key factors. The first is what God is accomplishing for us:

> He who began a good work in you *will* perfect it until the day of Christ Jesus.
>
> Philippians 1:6 (emphases mine)

> For if while we were enemies we *were* reconciled to God through the death of his Son, much more, having been reconciled, we *shall be* saved by His life.
>
> Romans 5:10 (emphases mine)

The second key is what we must accomplish—not *earn*—for ourselves:

> Work out your salvation with fear and trembling, for it is God who is at work in you, both to will and to work for His good pleasure.
>
> Philippians 2:12-13

> Discipline yourself for the purpose of godliness.
>
> 1 Timothy 4:7

For a moment, let's review the first three Books of *Mere Christianity*.

In Book 1, we saw that humans around the world are plagued by a curious sense of right and wrong. The phenomenon is universal and, contrary to our hopes and wishes otherwise, difficult to explain away. Furthermore, there are only a limited number of possible explanations for this internal 'ought.' Last of all, there is one other provoking fact about this 'ought' or Law of Human Nature: none of us live up to its standard. Thus, we cannot escape from it (it is within us) and we cannot live up to it (there is cause to be concerned).[55]

In Book 2, we are given a very odd solution—mind you, this is *the* Christian solution—to this problem: we are given a new life! We are not given, "Oh, let's just set aside the Law" or "Here are a few helpful tips on how to pass the test or how to live up to the requirements of the inner Law." No, the solution is straightforward: "new life." Period.

Now this brings us to Book 3 and—okay, I'll say it—twelve *long* chapters on morality! Lewis tells us that "moral rules are directions for running the human machine...to prevent a breakdown, or a strain, or a friction" and that a proper understanding of morality involves three parts or three areas where we human beings go amiss: outside ourselves in our social relationships; inside ourselves in our thoughts and emotions; and in the context of our purpose or relationship to the *power* that made us.[56]

We are then presented with a number of vices (or sins) and their opposing virtues (loosely summarized on the next page):

Vice (Sin)	Virtue
Imprudence: foolishness	Prudence: commonsense, think-then-act
Intemperance: gluttony, indulgence	Temperance: moderation
Injustice: dishonesty, prejudice	Justice: honesty, fairness
Cowardice: faintheartedness	Fortitude: courage, perseverance
Greed	Giving
'Christendom' minded: society focused	'Kingdom' minded: God focused
Self minded: 'raw material' focused	Spiritually minded: virtue focused
Fornication: lust & sex outside marriage	Chastity: abstinence
Adultery: infidelity	Fidelity: faithfulness in marriage
Unforgiving: grudge holding, retaliatory	Forgiveness: releasing debt
Pride: the sin of all sins	Humility
Unloving: indifference, affection only	Charity: Christian love & affection
Hopelessness: temporal futility & despair	Hope: longing for the eternal
Mood-driven: emotion, imagination	Faith 1: holds to what reason has accepted
Sin management: break own habits	Faith 2: exchanging habits

Last of all, Lewis does something startling! He tells us, in the final two chapters of Book 3, what was *actually* behind his ten previous chapters by citing what two *real* discoveries will be made if these virtues are *practiced*. The first is that we will fail!! We cannot be as virtuous (or good) as we are striving to be—we just cannot do it even though the desire is there. This leads to the second discovery: every faculty we have—thinking, moving, and so on—comes moment by moment from God! In fact, according to Lewis, making these two discoveries is so stupendous that, for the discoverer, his *real life has finally begun*—he is finally awake and *now* God can really get to work in him or her!

Stop, stop! What is Lewis talking about? If you are like me, two questions have probably popped into your thoughts: 1) Talking about practicing the virtues of "old writers" is very quaint, but is it even biblical? And 2) What is the difference between the 'ought' or Law and virtues or "directions for running the human machine"—if they are the same, aren't we just returning to Book 1? The answer to the first question is, "Yes, virtues are biblical." We see them scattered throughout scripture:

> "Finally, brethren, whatever is true, whatever is honorable, whatever is right, whatever is lovely, whatever is pure, whatever is lovely, whatever is of good repute, if there is any excellence and if anything worthy of praise, dwell on these things. The things you have learned and received and heard and seen in me, practice these things, and the God of peace will be with you."
>
> Philippians 4:8-9

"For by these He has granted to us His precious and magnificent promises, so that by them you may become partakers of the divine nature, having escaped the corruption that is in the world by lust. Now for this very reason also, applying all diligence, in your faith supply moral excellence, and in your moral excellence, knowledge, and in your knowledge, self-control, and in your self-control, perseverance, and in your perseverance, godliness, and in your godliness, brotherly kindness, and in your brotherly kindness, love. For if these qualities are yours and are increasing, they render you neither useless nor unfruitful in the true knowledge of our Lord Jesus Christ."

2 Peter 1:4-8

Even in the O.T., if, as I do, you believe that David—who claimed he had eternal life (Psalm 21:4, 133:3) and who Paul used as an example of justification apart from the Law (Romans 4:5-7)—had been saved by faith, we can see a fine list of virtues in his Psalm 15.

> O Lord, who may abide in Your tent
> Who may dwell on Your holy hill?
> He who walks with integrity, and works righteousness,
> And speaks truth in his heart.
> He does not slander with his tongue,
> Nor does evil to his neighbor,
> Nor takes up a reproach against his friend;
> In whose eyes a reprobate is despised,
> But who honors those who fear the Lord;
> He swears to his own hurt and does not change;
> He does not put out money at interest,
> Nor does he take a bribe against the innocent.
> He who does these things will never be shaken.

Psalm 15:1-5 (a Psalm of David)

Note that this handful of virtues is enough to authorize access to God's tent or presence, but 613 requirements were needed through the Mosaic Law.

So then, our second question: what is the difference between the Law and virtues? While many virtues are indistinguishable from individual statutes of the Mosaic Law, their purposes are not. Whereas the ultimate purpose of the Law led to the *putting in* of the living Christ within our dead Adam lives, the ultimate purpose of the virtues is the *putting off* of our dead Adam lives in order to bring out the living Christ life.[57] The following chart from Romans 1-8 may help clarify the role of the Law in moving us from *incompatible to compatible* and the role of the virtues (putting off or reckoning as dead) in moving us from *compatible* to *intimate*. If not, please just skip it.

GOD'S LIFE (IN CHRIST)
ROMANS 8:1-39
THE LAW OF THE SPIRIT OF LIFE HAS
LIBERATED US FROM THE LAW OF SIN AND
DEATH AND FULFILLED THE LAW OR 'OUGHT'

INTIMATE

Made Dead to (Adam's) Deadness
[Law or 'Ought' Fugue = Lethargy]
ROMANS 7:14-25

Made Dead to Sin
[Law or 'Ought' Forsaken = License]
ROMANS 6:1-23

Made Dead to the Law
[Law or 'Ought' Feigned = Legalism]
ROMANS 7:1-13

COMPATIBLE

**GOD'S GRACE
(EXITING ADAM)**

Law Cannot Produce Righteousness
[God's Law = All are Condemned]
ROMANS 3:1-20

Condemned by Approval of Lawlessness
[No Law or 'Ought' = Lawlessness]
ROMANS 1:1-32

Condemned by Being Sayers Not Doers
[Own Law or 'Ought' = Self-righteousness]
ROMANS 2:1-29
JEW   GENTILE

INCOMPATIBLE

**GOD'S WRATH
(IN ADAM)**

156

Now, let's return to the biblical doctrine of Transformation. The Bible also refers to this as "putting off" and "putting on" (2 Corinthian 5:17, Galatians 2:19-20, Ephesians 4:22-24; Colossians 3:8-10). I call this *changing from being compatible with God to being intimate with Him*. What it is called, however, is far less important than how it is practiced. A common but mistaken way of practicing this has been referred to as "Sin Management."[58] Essentially, this way does not recognize the "saved by Christ's death" aspect of what Christ is accomplishing in us but simply allows the old Adam-man to run the show:

Sin Management	Putting Off & Putting On
No transformation of old self is needed but usually only a self that *now* "knows better"	Involves the transformation of old sinful self into a new creature
Sin is managed by old self's own *internal* notions of 'right' & 'wrong' and/or by conforming to the *external* 'norms' of church, society, traditions and so on	Through practice, as the old sin-nature self is identified as crucified with Christ, a new self identity emerges that is associated with Christ's risen life

Other than not being scriptural, what is the major problem with the old Adam-man's independent efforts to patch up its own sins? Not dependently working out what God is working within us will continuously prevent us from coming to know Him in a way that can only be known by becoming like Him:

> The apostle denies that anyone actually knows Christ who has not learned to put off the old man, corrupt with deceitful lust, and to put on the Christ. External knowledge of Christ is found to be only a false and dangerous make-believe, however eloquently and freely lip servants may talk about the gospel.
>
> John Calvin
> *Golden Booklet of the True Christian Life,* 1550

The conviction has grown steadily upon me that union with Christ, rather than justification or election or eschatology, or indeed any of the other great apostolic themes, is the real clue to an understanding of Paul's thoughts and experience...It is perhaps also a point worthy of remark that, while *justification and reconciliation* undoubtedly look forward and contain in germ all the harvest of the Spirit that is to come, yet—by the very nature of the terms themselves—they carry with them, and can never quite shake off, a memory of the old life left behind; their positive implies a negative; they speak of a transition, a break, an end and a beginning; and their brightness has a dark background to set it off. *Union with Christ,* on the other hand, means the steady, unbroken glory of a quality of life which shines by its own light, because it is essentially supernatural; allows no hint of any negative, because 'the fullness of God' is in it; and knows no before or after, because it is already eternal.

James S. Stewart
A Man in Christ, 1935

It is the change from being confident about our own efforts to the state in which we despair of doing anything for ourselves and leave it to God...The sense in which a Christian leaves it to God is that he puts all his trust in Christ: trusts that Christ will somehow share with him the perfect human obedience which He carried out from His birth to His crucifixion; that Christ will make the man more like Himself and, in a sense, make good his deficiencies. In Christian language, He will share His 'sonship' with us, will make us, like Himself, 'sons of God'...

C.S. Lewis
Mere Christianity, 1952

Appendix 11:
New Men: Theological Gas or Reality?

Already the new men are dotted here and there all over the earth. Some, as I have admitted, are still hardly recognizable: but others can be recognized. Every now and then one meets them...They begin where most of us leave off. They are, I say, recognizable; but you must know what to look for. They will not be very like the idea of 'religious people'...When you have recognized one of them, you will recognize the next one much more easily

...you must not imagine that the new men are, in the ordinary sense, all alike...Sameness is to be found most among the most 'natural' men, not among those who surrender to Christ. How monotonously alike all the great tyrants and conquerors have been; how gloriously different are the saints.

C.S. Lewis
Mere Christianity, 1952

I once met the elderly proprietor of a small art gallery by the name of Dr. William Wallner. A family member pointed out that he was listed in *Who's Who* for both photography and *religion*. The latter was for having led over 3000 Jews to Christ in Europe after WWII. I could not resist asking him if he had ever met C.S. Lewis and I will never forget his response. Without any elaboration he simply locked his smiling, recollecting eyes on mine and replied, "Yes! There was something different about him!"

Many years later, following a church service, I was stopped by acquaintance who recommended I go to a Sunday School room to hear a visiting seminar teacher. The only reason given for the recommendation was, "There is something different about him!" I had never heard of the teacher and had no idea what his seminar was about, but when he began to speak, it quickly became clear that what he was teaching was what he was living. An unmistakable quality of deep, calm peace surrounded him that was almost thick or heavy. I had been around the block and read through the entire Bible enough times to be more than a neophyte, but when Dallas Willard brought forth Scriptures about personal discipleship under Jesus leading to Christlikeness, I was amazed—how had I never grasped this before? And was I only imagining it or was an in-Christ-present-with-God-life standing right before me?

From that time on, I began to rethink my faith, to appreciate the connection between my salvation with my spirituality, and to seek more deeply "His purpose...[of becoming] conformed to the image of His Son, that He might be the first born among *many* brethren" (Romans 8:28-29) During times of discouragement in this process, I have often been encouraged by the "great cloud of witness" God has given to us, those new men "dotted here and there all over the earth." Below is a sampling of that witness—not only from Biblical but also post-biblical accounts—to reaffirm that the people mentioned in Scripture are no different than us and God's purpose then is no different than it is today.

The Biblical Witness

And it came about when Moses was coming down from Mount Sinai...that the skin of his face shone because of his speaking with Him.

Exodus 34:29

There is a man in your kingdom in whom is a spirit of the holy gods; and in the days of your father, illumination, insight and wisdom like the wisdom of the gods were found in him.

Daniel 5:11

And He was transfigured before them; and His face shone like the sun...

Matthew 17:2

But some men...rose up and argued with Stephen. And yet they were unable to cope with the wisdom and Spirit with which he was speaking...all who were sitting in the Council saw his face like the face of an angel.

Acts 6:9-10, 15

When the crowds saw what Paul had done, they shouted..."The gods have come down to us in human form!"

Acts 14:11

The Post-Biblical Witness

What is that which gleams through me and smites my heart without wounding? I am both a-shudder and aglow. A-shudder, in so far as I am unlike it, aglow in so far as I am like it.

Augustine
self description in *Confessions*, 400A.D.

Of this blest man, let this just praise be given: heaven was in him, before he was in heaven.

Izaak Walton
description of Richard Sibbs after his 1635 death

Further, the Lord did also lead me into the mystery of union with the Son of God...By this also was my faith in him, as my righteousness, the more confirmed in me; for if he and I were one, then his righteousness was mine, his victory also mine. Now I could see myself in heaven and earth at once, in heaven by my Christ, by my head, by my righteousness and life, though on earth by my body or person...Now was God and Christ continually before my face...the glory of the holiness of God did at this time break me to pieces...

John Bunyan
Grace Abounding to the Chief of Sinners, 1666

For more than forty years, this brother's [self reference] principal endeavor has been to stay as close as possible to God, doing, saying, and thinking nothing that might displease Him...This brother has become so accustomed to God's divine presence that he relies on it for help on all sorts of occasions. His soul has been filled with a constant inner joy that is sometimes so overwhelming, he feels compelled to do what may seem to some as childish things, in order to prevent the feeling from becoming too intense.

Brother Lawrence (Nicholas Herman), 1614-91
from *The Practice of the Presence of God*

As I read these words [1Timothy 1:17], there came into my soul and was, as it were, diffused through it a sense of the glory of the Divine Being, a new sense, quite different from anything I ever experienced before. The sense I had of divine things would often of a sudden kindle up, as it were, a sweet burning in my heart, and ardor of soul, that I know not how to express. Not long after I first began to experience these things, I walked abroad alone, in a solitary place in my father's pasture, for contemplation. And as I was walking there, and looking up on the sky and clouds, there came into my mind so sweet a sense of the glorious majesty and grace of God that I know not how to express it...an awful sweetness, a high, and great, and holy gentleness. After this my sense of divine things gradually increased and became more and more lively, and had more of that inward sweetness. The appearance of everything was altered; there seemed to be, as it were, a calm sweet cast or appearance of divine glory in almost everything. God's excellency, His wisdom, His purity and love, seemed to appear in everything...

Jonathan Edwards, 1703-1758
from "The Memoirs of Jonathan Edwards"
in *The Works of Jonathan Edwards*

When I saw Mr. Whitefield come upon the Scaffold [that had been erected for the sermon] he Lookt almost angelic...for he was Clothed with authority from the Great God; and a sweet sollome solemnity sat upon his brow and my hearing him preach, gave me a heart wound...

> Nathan Cole, common Connecticut farmer
> Diary entry after George Whitefield's sermon
> Middletown, Connecticut, 1740

Mr. Taylor plunged into his story. In characteristic fashion—his hands behind his back—he walked up and down the room exclaiming, "Oh, Mr. Judd, God has made me a new man! God has made me a new man!"...He is a joyous man now [Mr. Judd recorded], a bright happy Christian. He had been a toiling, burdened one before, with latterly not much rest of soul. It was resting in Jesus now, and letting Him do the work—which made all the difference. Whenever he spoke in meetings after that, a new power seemed to flow from him, and in the practical things of life a new peace possessed him. Troubles did not worry him as before. He cast everything on God in a new way, and gave more time to prayer. Instead of working late at night, he began to go to bed earlier, rising at 5 A. M. to give time to Bible study and prayer (often two hours) before the work of the day began.

It was the exchanged life that had come to him—the life that is indeed "No longer I." Six months earlier he had written, "I have continually to mourn that I follow at such a distance and learn so slowly to imitate my Master." There was no thought of imitation now! It was in blessed reality "Christ liveth in me."

> Hudson Taylor's 1869 transformation
> in *Hudson Taylor's Spiritual Secret*,

I cannot describe it, I seldom refer to it, it is almost too sacred an experience to name...I can only say God revealed Himself to me, and I had such an experience of His love that I had to ask Him to stay His hand. I went to preaching again. The sermons were not different; I did not present any new truths; and yet hundreds were converted. I would not now be placed back where I was before that blessed experience if you gave me all the world...

> Moody's description of his life-transformation
> A. P. Fitt's *The Shorter Life of D. L. Moody*, 1900

As for the man: he is about 52, of humble origin (there are still traces of cockney in his voice), ugly as a chimpanzee but so radiant (he emanates more love than any man I have ever known) that as soon as he begins talking whether in private or in a lecture he is transfigured and looks like an angel. He sweeps some people quite off their feet and has many disciples...He works in the Oxford University

Press. In spite of his "angelic" quality he is also quite an earthy person and when Warnie, Tolkien, he and I meet for our pint in a pub in Broad Street, the fun is often so fast and furious that the company probably thinks we're talking bawdy when in fact we're v. likely talking Theology. He is married and, I think, youthfully in love with his wife still.

C.S. Lewis
personal description of Charles Williams, 1944

[H]e always seemed to me to diffuse an atmosphere of happiness, of joy in every smallest event in life, and of deep gratitude for the mere fact that he was alive...He was one of the very few men that I have met to whom his God was real and ever close to him.

S. Payne Best
description of Dietrich Bonhoeffer, Nazi prison, 1945
in *The Venlo Incident*, 1950

Tozer knelt by his chair, took off his glasses and laid them on the chair. Resting on his bent ankles, he clasped his hands together, raised his face with his eyes closed and began: 'O God, we are before Thee.' With that, there came a rush of God's presence that filled the room. We both worshipped in silent ecstasy and wonder and adoration. I've never forgotten that moment, and I don't want to forget it.

Raymond McAfee, *Reflections*, 1987
personal description of praying with A.W. Tozer

Appendix 12:
C.S. Lewis's Spiritual Secret

C.S. Lewis spent the greater part of his adult life in academia where his usual acquaintances consisted of a small group of fellow academicians and students. He did not own a car or drive. He attended the same church near his home—but was probably unknown to most parishioners—or at the Dean's Chapel while in academic session. He was neither an ordained pastor nor a trained theologian. He died in relative obscurity. Nevertheless, he was an incredibly influential Christian:

> During his 1941-44 BBC radio broadcasts, Lewis began to receive significant amounts of mail. He felt obligated to personally answer each letter in writing. The actual number of letters he wrote is unknown. Later in life his brother Warnie began to help out with some of the volume by typing responses: the number of letters recorded on Warnie's typewriter alone was over ten thousand.

> While she was an undergraduate in Oxford between 1942 and 1945, Rachel Trickett noted that "Lewis was the uncrowned king not only of the English faculty but of the whole university. His influence was widespread through the Socratic Club, an undergraduate society for the dissemination of philosophical and theological ideas."

> In 1947, C.S. Lewis made the cover of *Time* Magazine, very uncommon for religious personalities even back then.

> In 1958, a survey asked 415 missionaries, "Who was the most influential person in your becoming a missionary?" Fifty percent responded, "C.S. Lewis."

> Sheldon Vanauken published *A Severe Mercy* in 1977. In it, he recorded the numerous letters from and—after traveling from American to England—meetings with Lewis that led to his and his wife's own conversions to Christ.

> In his 1991 book, *Disciplines of a Godly Man*, Kent Hughes surveyed many well-known, contemporary Christian theologians, pastors and authors (Chuck Colson, James Boice, Carl F. H. Henry, Calvin Miller, Eugene Peterson, R.C. Sproul, Chuck Swindoll, etc.) with "What are the five books, secular or sacred, which have influenced you the most?" Apart from the Bible, the most frequently cited book was *Mere Christianity* by C.S. Lewis.

While researching *Seeking the Secret Place: the Spiritual Formation of C.S. Lewis* (2004), Lyle Dorsett interviewed hundreds of people who individually stated that Lewis's writings had led them to Christ. In the Selected Bibliography of Dorsett's book, besides the nearly sixty books that were written *by* Lewis, there are over ninety listed that were written *about* him.

William Lane Craig reports that Lewis's "books have sold more than 100 million copies worldwide" in *On Guard: Defending Your Faith with Reason and Precision* (2010).

Decades after his death, even the secular world has taken note of Lewis. In 1993, Hollywood released *Shadowlands*, a biographical account of Lewis and Joy Gresham's relationship starring Anthony Hopkins and Debra Winger. Also Disney has had excellent box office success with its film adaptations of Lewis's *The Chronicles of Narnia*.

Without a question, then, Lewis was very influential as a Christian. What is a question, however, is: "How?" How did he become so influential? What was his secret? I do not mean the secret to his popularity, but the *spiritual secret* to his influence upon others for Christ.

The answer to this may not be what the ordinary Christian would expect. Certainly, Lewis was recognized as having an extremely intelligence and creative mind. He also was situated in academia at very prestigious universities—Oxford and later Cambridge—where his thinking would have been constantly challenged and sharpened. Furthermore he did not face the commitments and responsibilities of marriage and parenting until he was in his late fifties. No doubt, these were all important factors but they are not the whole story because, throughout history, there have been many other intelligent, unmarried Christian academicians who were *not* nearly as influential.

The spiritual secret behind the Christian influence of C.S. Lewis rests with one thing: *he took transformation seriously*—he cultivated his desire for intimacy with the Almighty, he put effort into his call to become a *new* man. The creative, playful and yet sober explanations we find in *Mere Christianity* are not those of a man with only a hypothetical knowledge of the process of transformation, but an experiential knowledge.

For specific details about the actual "spiritual disciplines" Lewis practiced in his life, I highly recommend Lyle Dorsett's well-researched *Seeking the Secret Place: the Spiritual Formation of C.S. Lewis*. But for the purposes of the present discussion, I will only allude to a select few of the practices.

Though Lewis loathed the sectarianism divisions within Christianity and felt that a deeper, more genuine, more "Baxterian" *mere* Christianity would erase many of the differences, "there is no way to understand the growth and strength of this great twentieth soul without seeing him in the caring hands of his spiritual mother, the Anglican Church."[59] My point here is not to discuss the merits and minuses of the Anglican Church but rather to understand what it provided for Lewis to grow and deepen as a Christian.[60] There were, I believe, three essential things:

1) The use of the Bible and *The Common Book of Prayer*

2) A spiritual mentor or guide

3) Specific daily disciplines

First of all, while all Protestant denominations uniformly adhere to salvation through the cross of Christ, how they view Scripture as a guide for living varies. A common and unfortunate use of the Bible in today's church is its *non-use*. The Anglican use of *The Common Book of Prayer* did two things for Lewis. One was that it kept *weekly* church services *liturgical*—mundanely reviewing essential passages of the Old Testament, Psalms, the New Testaments and the Gospels—and not *novel* which far too often has only an entertainment value. People should not go to church to be entertained, but, as Lewis held, "They go to use the service or, if you prefer, to enact it. Every service is a structure of acts and words..."[61] If nothing else, the essential benefit for Lewis was a repetitive ongoing exposure to Scripture. The other was that it also *daily* kept him reading and reviewing Scripture while not in church throughout the year.

Second, though previously outlawed, in the 1800's nuns and monks who voluntarily chose celibate lives were allowed back into the Anglican Church. One group of monks, the "Crowley Fathers," lived near to Oxford, only a short distance for Lewis's rooms.

> Beginning in the summer of 1940, this gifted writer, teacher, and intellect fell under conviction that he needed a spiritual director. Such a decision came only after an agonizing season of prayer...It is doubtful that anyone had a more profound impact on Lewis's spiritual development in the spiritually formative years from 1949 to 1952 than Father Walter Adams...For nearly twelve years C.S. Lewis walked the short trek from his rooms at Magdalen College, Oxford, to the immediately adjacent village of Cowley, where the Cowley Fathers lived and ministered...Unless one of them was out of town, Lewis met with Walter Adams nearly every week. From this humble and relatively unknown monk, the increasingly famous Oxford don who hungered to grow in holiness learned to follow several essential paths to an increasingly Christlike life.[62]

Third, Lewis was given a number of spiritual disciplines by Walter Adams which were monitored and adjusted as needed. These included daily prayer, weekly confession and Communion, and reading the "daily office."[63] But one other important discipline was assigned to Lewis by Adams that was outside the usual order of *The Book of Common Prayer*: "praying through all 150 Psalms each month."[64]

For many of us, the practicality in today's busy world of a weekly liturgical worship or daily lifestyle—Anglican or non-Anglican—is beyond our reach. Likewise, the availability of a seasoned spiritual mentor-guide—although desirable—is also implausible. However, *praying* the Psalms, as a personal daily spiritual-discipline is well within all our grasps. Allow me to share a few other voices on this:

> "Lord, teach us Lord to pray"...The child learns to speak because his father speaks to him. He learns the speech of his father...By means of the speech of the Father in heaven, his children learn to speak with him. Repeating God's own words after him, we begin to pray to him. We ought to speak to God and he wants to hear us, not in the false and confused speech of our heart, but in the clear and pure speech which God has spoken to us in Jesus Christ...Now there is in Holy Scripture a book which is distinguished from all other books of the Bible by the fact that it contains only prayers. It is at first very surprising that there is a prayerbook in the Bible. The Holy Scripture is the Word of God. But prayers are the words of men. How then do prayers get into the Bible. Let us make no mistake about it, the Bible is the Word of God even in the Psalms. Then are these prayers to God also God's own words? That seems difficult to understand. We grasp it only when we remember that we can learn true prayer only from Jesus Christ, from the word of the Son of God, who lives with men, to God the Father, who lives in eternity...In his mouth the word of man becomes the Word of God, and if we pray his prayer with him, the Word of God becomes once again the word of man.
>
> Dietrich Bonhoeffer
> *Psalms: The Prayer Book of the Bible*, 1940

Why has the Church always considered the Psalms her most perfect book of prayer?...the Psalms are the songs of men who *knew who God was*. If we are to pray well, we too must discover the Lord to whom we speak, and if we use the Psalms in our prayers we will stand a better chance of sharing in the discovery which lies hidden in their words for all generations. For God has willed to make Himself known to us in the mystery of the Psalms...The whole Psalter has always been regarded by the Church...as though it were a summary and a compendium of all that God has revealed. In other words the Psalms contain in themselves all the

Old and New Testaments, the whole Mystery of Christ...[The Church] recommends the Psalms in order to have the mind of Christ.

Thomas Merton
Praying the Psalms, 1956

If you bury yourself in Psalms, you emerge knowing God and understanding life...We learn from the psalms how to think and act in reference to God. We drink in God and God's world from them. They provide a vocabulary for living Godward, one inspired by God himself. They show us who God is, and that expands and lifts and directs our minds and our hearts.

Dallas Willard
The Divine Conspiracy, 1998

By praying the Psalms back to God, we learn to pray in tune with the Father, Son and Holy Spirit...There is no better place in all of Scripture than the Psalms to learn to be with God and to see with the eyes of faith the face of the One who longs to form us fully in his image. But the Psalms can be hard; they often stretch and perplex us as they teach. How could it be otherwise? The Psalms are God's prayer book, and they teach us to talk to God in his own language.

Ben Patterson
God's Prayer Book, 2008

Praying the Psalms is as old as Christianity itself. As a practice, it involves effort and discipline. Nevertheless, in my 35 plus years as an evangelical Christian, I have never found another single daily practice that has held me as close to God and allowed sight of what He was engineering in my life as I have by praying the Psalms.[65] To any believer seeking to be more intimate with God, seeking to better exercise the mind of Christ, it is difficult to recommend a better means.

1 See Abraham Maslow, *Religions, Values and Peak Experiences* (Columbus: Ohio State Univ. Press, 1965); Marghanita Laski, *Ecstasy* (Indiana University Press, 1962); Andrew Greeley, *Ecstasy: a Way of Knowing.* (New Jersey: Prentice-Hall, 1974); even Albert Einstein acknowledged this experience: "...the cosmic religious experience is the strongest and the noblest driving force behind scientific research." (New York Times, 1930)

2 C.S. Lewis, *Surprised by Joy* (New York: Harcourt Brace Jovanovich, 1955), p. 16-18

3 Dallas Willard, *Hearing God.* (Downers Grove, IL: InterVarsity Press, 1993), p. 194

4 Harry Blamires, *The Christian Mind* (Ann Arbor: Servant Books, 1963 [1978]), p. 13

5 *ibid*, p. 78

6 *ibid*, p. 79-80

7 C.S. Lewis, *Mere Christianity* (New York: Macmillan, 1952 [1980]), p. 78

8 Acts 9:30-31, NASB

9 1 Corinthians 2:2-5, NASB

10 C.S. Lewis, *Mere Christianity,* p. 174

11 *ibid*, p. 199

12 Foster, *Celebration of Discipline* (New York: HarperCollins, 1978) p. 1

13 C.S. Lewis, *The Abolition of Man* [Riddell Memorial Lectures, University of Durham] (New York: McMillan, 1947, Paperback Edition, 1965), p.95-121—Introductory Comments & Parts I-VIII from Appendix: Illustrations of the Tao

14 Flow Chart is adapted and modified from Peter Kreeft, *Why Debate the Existence of God?* in J. P. Moreland & Kai Nielsen, *Does God Exist?* (Amherst, NY: Prometheus, 1993) p.15

15 Definitions are provided to explain the components of the chart. They are not derived from any single reference source.

16 Don Richardson, *Eternity in their Hearts* (Ventura, CA: Regal, 1981) p.. 137-8

17 *ibid*, p. 142-3

18 *ibid*, p. 143

19 Bolton Davidheiser, *Evolution and Christian Faith* (Grand Rapids: Baker Book House, 1969), p. 350-4

20 Edward Tylor, *Primitive Culture: Researches into the Development of Mythology, Philosophy, Religion, Art and Custom*, 1865; also Primitive Culture, 1871 [See Don Richardson, Eternity in their Hearts, p. 118-122]

21 Wilhelm Schmidt, *Primitive Revelation* (St. Louis: R. Herder, 1939) [See Don Richardson, Eternity in their Hearts, p. 120-125]

22 Don Richardson, *Eternity in their Hearts*, p. 16-20

23 *ibid*, p. 22-23

24 *ibid*, p. 48-50

25 *ibid*, p. 50-55

26 *ibid*, p. 37-43

27 *ibid*, p. 80-81

28 *ibid*, p. 81-82

29 *ibid*, p. 65-76

30 *ibid*, p. 76-77

31 *ibid*, p. 80

32 *ibid*, p. 79

33 *ibid*, p. 77

34 *ibid*, p. 55-56

35 *ibid*, p. 80

36 *ibid*, p. 55

37 *ibid*, p. 110-112

38 *ibid*, p. 109-112

39 *ibid*, p. 30-37

40 Steve Saint, *End of the Spear* (Carole Stream, IL: Tyndale House, 2005)

41 Winston Churchill, Speech, October 22, 1945, in R. Langworth, *Churchill By Himself* (New York, Public Affairs: 2008) p. 13

42 ibid. Speech, March 2, 1947, p. 29

43 Margaret Thatcher, Interview, *This Week*, Feb.5, 1976

44 Ronald Sider, *The Scandal of the Evangelical Conscience* (Grand Rapids, Baker Books: 2006) p. 21

45 C.S. Lewis, *Mere Christianity* (New York, HarperCollins, 2001) p. 86

46 *ibid*, p. 82

47 Malcolm Muggeridge, The End of Christendom (Grand Rapids: Wm. Eerdmans: 1980) p. 1-34

48 *ibid*. p. 35-62

49 Malcolm Muggeridge, *Jesus, The Man Who Lives* (New York: Harper & Row, 1975) p.61

50 *ibid*, p.61

51 Larry Crabb, *The Safest Place on Earth* (Nashville: Word Publishing, 1999) p. 161

52 Craig Ellison, *From Stress to Well-Being* (Eugene: Wipf and Stock Publishers, 2003) p. 7

53 *ibid*, Chapters 1-12

54 C.S. Lewis, *Mere Christianity* (New York: HarperCollins, 1952 [2001]) p. 92

55 Was there a capacity to know right a wrong before the Fall? To some degree, though not much is revealed, there had to be. The permissible or good things Adam and Eve could do included naming animals, working the garden, eating from the fruit trees, running around naked and procreating. The one and only forbidden or wrong or bad thing they could do was eat from the tree of knowledge of good and evil. What happened to Adam and Eve as a result of the Fall was not the introduction of a new knowledge capacity but a change in the underlying basis for that capacity: they changed from a God-based knowledge of right and wrong or good and evil to a self-based knowledge of right and wrong or good and evil.

56 After the Fall, Adam cited perceived flaws with Eve (for providing him with fruit from the forbidden tree), with himself (for realizing he was naked) and with God (for giving him Eve and making him naked). These are the three moral areas with which we have troubles: 1) outside ourselves in our social relationships; 2) inside ourselves in our thoughts and emotions; and 3) in the context of our purpose or relationship to the power that made us.

57 The Law brings knowledge of sin (Romans 3:19, 7:7) and power for sin to expose our deadness to God (1 Corinthians 15:56; Romans 5:12-14, 7:9); this, in turn, invokes His wrath (Romans 4:15). The Law was added to restrain our transgressions (Galatians 3:19), to act as a guardian (Galatians 3:24) and to point us to Christ who initiated our release from the death-curse of the Law (Galatians 3:13). Practicing the virtues or, as they are sometimes called, spiritual disciplines have no inherent or meritorious value in themselves. They counter sin merely by taking what Christ's death has already accomplished and "reckoning it" or "regarding it as true" relative to specific sins in ourselves. Properly practiced, effort is not applied to patching up but rather to putting off our old Adam-man.

58 Dallas Willard, *The Divine Conspiracy* (New York: HarperCollins, 1998) p. 35-59

59 Lyle Dorsett, *Seeking the Secret Place: the Spiritual Formation of C.S. Lewis* (Grand Rapids: Brazos Press, 2004) p. 71

60 The issue is this: If your church held to all the right doctrines, if it had a wonderful pastor and staff, if it was housed in a clean and comfortable building or complex of buildings, if it was within a reasonable and safe locality—in other words, if your church was pretty much perfect—yet, year after year, it failed to produce much more than 'spiritual zeros' in terms of spiritual maturity, would you continue to fellowship there?

61 C.S. Lewis, *Letters to Malcolm: Chiefly on Prayer* (London: Geoffrey Bles, 1964) p.12

62 Lyle Dorsett, *Seeking the Secret Place*, p. 85, 88, 92, 93

63 See *The Common Book of Prayer* (1662, 1789—multiple editions available)

64 Lyle Dorsett, Seeking the Secret Place, p. 96

65 As a discipline for exercising the mind of Christ, I pray—not read—through about three to five Psalms every day to the Lord. During my prayers, if something jumps off the page at me—a verse or even just a phrase within a verse—I jot it down. I finish my prayers by "piggy backing" on my own personal prays and supplications for myself and others on my list to the Lord. I then take what I jotted down and spend time repeating it in my mind, thinking about it, trying to understand it from different viewpoints with requests for wisdom and insight—this is meditating NOT memorizing. Finally I take that phrase or verse into my day, written down on a card or scrap of paper, and use it as a reminder to practice His presence or set my mind on the Lord. Depending on my day, I may re-attend to Him via the verse every 5 minutes or every hour. Some days I am able to attend to Him for long stretches at a time.

Made in the USA
Monee, IL
08 January 2020